A Worldwide *Sisterhood*

You Are Distinct & Different

compiled by
Kay West

A Worldwide Sisterhood: You Are Distinct & Different

"*In this book you will find many prayerfully sought out understandings that will speak to your heart through the Spirit. Each of these sister authors share the things of her heart, the hard-won clarity for many questions we universally seek answers for as we work our way through this challenging human existence. As you read, you will undoubtedly feel reassured that you are not alone in the things you experience. You will find thoughts that will stretch your thinking in a way that will necessitate further pondering and prayer and repeated reading. You will find many examples of how to apply scriptures and the words of our modern-day leaders to the problems we face. Prepare to feast upon the words of Christ through the eyes and experiences of sisters just like you.*"

- Dixie Davis, Raymond, Alberta, Canada

"*This is a beautiful compilation of stories, experiences, and thoughts from real women. Reading this will leave you uplifted, grateful, and full of purpose. We all have mountains to climb, as Kay says it, but it is a reminder that the Lord will guide us through it.*"

Angie Chandler, Mendon, Utah, USA
comefollowmefhe.com @comefollowmefhe

"*A Worldwide Sisterhood: You Are Distinct and Different is a wonderful collection of stories from women around the world-- stories filled with hope and grit and love for the Savior. The spirit it brings will leave you feeling inspired to draw closer to Jesus Christ and better understand the divine potential that lies within you!*"

Annie Cockcroft, Oak Ridge, North Carolina, USA

Acknowledgements

This isn't how it's done, but I cannot let one more page turn without saying thank you.

First, I want to express the most sincere gratitude to every single one of the author contributors in this book. Audra, Becky, Chelsea, Darla, Jodi, Lauren, Renee, Rhonda, Starr, and Tiffany. These amazing women of faith not only inspire me daily but also have been a huge source of strength and encouragement throughout this whole process. I love these women. I admire these women. I am forever grateful for these women.

All of my deepest gratitude goes to Dixie and Annie. You ladies helped me to move forward when I didn't think I would be able to. Your amazing insight, suggestions, and encouragement got us over the finish line and there are no words that accurately express my love for you both.

Thank you, Audra, there is no way any of this would have happened without you.

Thank you to Brooke Romney, Julie Bristow, and Rhonna Farrer. You ladies have had the most profound influence on me. Thank you for all your help, love, encouragement, and guidance.

Thank you, Rhonda, for the cover photo and beautiful digital elements.

To all the amazing women I have met the past two years who are the inspiration for this. I am speaking to YOU.

Thank YOU!

You have no idea the love I truly have for each of you. Your light has been a source of true joy. Your light has been the pure light of Christ and your examples testify of Him. If you have had any interaction with me at all, no matter how large or what *you* believe may be small, I am speaking to *YOU*.

Thank you to my husband and children, for supporting everything single thing I do, every single day.

To everyone, just, thank you so much.

Your light is

distinct & different.

Together as
A WORLDWIDE
Sisterhood

our lights combine to
shine the light of

Christ

to the world in a
distinct & different way.

– Kay West –

Table of Contents

Introduction

We speak of peculiarity, uniqueness, and of being distinct & different.

But what does that mean?

What does it look like?

In a world that seems to be losing faith and hope, we must rise above and continue to share Christ, His message, and His light.

"We must stand and be visibly different.
Until we make that choice, we remain anonymous,
subject to the current of the meandering multitudes."[1]

---

[1] Kapp, Ardeth G. "Drifting, Dreaming, Directing," *At the Pulpit: 185 Years of Discourses by Latter-day Saint Women.* Intellectual Reserve, Inc.,2017, p.200.

How can we do this?

We can start by seeking Christ for ourselves.

Do you know Him? Do you know He is here with us today? Do you know He walks here, serves here, and loves here just as He did long ago?

He does all this through each of us. And as we come to know Him more, He will be able to continue to use your small efforts and magnify them into something visibly distinct & different.

I began *A Worldwide Sisterhood* because I felt something stirring inside me. I love the voices, faithfulness, and light of amazing women disciples who know their Savior, and strive to emulate Him in their daily lives.

I heard amazing voices from women around me. And I often heard the same voices. Voices I love, voices that teach, voices that lift.

And still I was missing *something*.

To be distinct & different, unique, and peculiar, I want to hear ALL voices.

YOUR voice.

Within this book you will find different voices from women around the world who are rising to our Savior's call! Some voices will resonate with you right now, some maybe not in this season, but a future season.

Whether you connect with a few or all of the voices contained in this book, my main hope is that this book will inspire YOU to understand that you are distinct & different, and YOU are needed!

Your voice, your example, your testimony, your faith, and your light.

YOU are needed right now, because I feel a movement.

I feel a movement among sister saints who want to be bold and stand immovable in their testimonies of Christ.

I feel a movement of women warriors who heed the battle cry and combat the enemy with unwavering faith and conviction in truth.

I feel a movement of women rising to their calling and purpose as a daughter of God.

I feel a movement of women willing to literally walk in the footsteps of their Savior and lift others.

I feel a movement of women willing to move mountains and conquer the cliffs of fear that may loom over them.

I feel a movement of women disciples who stand silent to hear Him and then stand ready to raise their voice loud and strong for Him.

I feel this movement everywhere.

It is a movement of faithful women who are fulfilling prophecy[2] and are rising to the call to be distinct & different.

There is something stirring in your soul, I know you have felt it, nudging you to act and do something you may not yet understand.

Maybe you are hesitant, a little afraid to stand alone, to rise up to fulfill what may at times feel a daunting task.

It's ok, you are not alone.

Look up, always look up. He will never fail you!

I know you have the strength within you to rise to the challenge!

When you do, and you stand visibly different, take a very brief look around.

You will no longer remain anonymous, you will rise distinct from meandering multitudes and see others have chosen to do the same.

You *are* distinct & different. You have something that needs to be shared. Never underestimate the influence your reach has, especially within the walls of your own home, and then beyond.

Because there is a distinct & different movement.

Through all of it, Christ is at the center. His peace, His mercy, His light, His love.

---

[2] Kimball, Spencer W. "The Role of Righteous Women," General Conference October 1979

And this is why we wrote this book. To remind *you* that you are distinct & different.

And YOU are needed.

Founder, A Worldwide Sisterhood

———1———
Starr Anderson

You Are Not Forgotten

"O Lord, do not be angry with thy servant because of his weakness..."[3] How often has this been my cry? These words, and others, spoken by the brother of Jared have always seemed to stir my soul. In fact, the Book of Ether, where these words are found, has become one of my favorite books within the Book of Mormon.

The first few chapters of Ether contain scripture blocks that sink deeply into my heart. Over time, the Lord has used various verses from the brother of Jared's story to provide me with very personal revelation and direction. For me, it was within the Book of Ether

---

[3] Ether 3:2, The Book of Mormon

where I first began to notice that the Lord can use the scriptures to provide guidance, answers, and patterns of truth.

In Ether, chapter 1 we learn that the brother of Jared, along with his family and friends, were led by the Lord to seek a land of promise. Jared's people were remembered when the Lord promised not to confound their language at the Tower of Babel. It would seem, they then wandered in the wilderness for four years before they were remembered again. That remembering would bring a chastisement from the Lord, "for he (the brother of Jared) remembered not to call upon the name of the Lord."[4] These people would then be commanded to build barges that would carry them across raging waters.

Knowing that there would be darkness in these vessels, the brother of Jared sought the Lord's counsel so that his people would not have to cross vast waters in blackness. The scriptures teach us that he "molted out of rock sixteen small stones...and he did carry them in his hands upon the top of the mount, and cried unto the Lord..."[5] The brother of Jared intended for these small and simple stones to provide the light he was seeking for their journey.

The brother of Jared's prayer can have a powerful impact on each of our lives. It is a prayer that perhaps we ourselves have uttered:

"O Lord, thou hast said that we must be encompassed about by the floods. Now behold, O Lord, and do not be angry with thy servant because of his weakness...we are unworthy before thee; because of the fall our natures have become evil continually...for these many years we have been in the wilderness...O Lord, look upon me in pity, and turn away thine anger from this thy people, and suffer not

---

[4] Ether 2:14, The Book of Mormon
[5] Ether 3:1, The Book of Mormon

2

that they shall go forth across this raging deep in darkness; but behold these things which I have molten out of the rock."[6]

Have you felt floods in your own life? Have you felt your weakness, unworthiness, or fallen nature? I believe these feelings can come to each of us throughout our mortal experience. I have found myself, like the brother of Jared, figuratively standing with outstretched arms, presenting to my Heavenly Father what seems like a meager offering: the stones of my efforts and desires. Perhaps my pleas have sounded very similar; "behold these *things*, for I do not know what else to call them. Please, I am trying, accept my efforts!"

My desire is to share with you my personal witness that the Lord accepts our offerings and he has not forgotten us. The Lord reveals himself to us, most often through the spirit, consistently and profoundly! My message to each of us is that no matter how lost we may feel, how deeply we want to be remembered, or how often our own experiences feel inadequate, the Lord remembers us! He comes to us! He can and will reveal himself to us!

The scriptures are laced with beautiful accounts that can teach us about the Lord's pattern of "showing up" in our lives. I hope you will fall in love with the sample of passages that follow. I hope by sharing my own experiences you will remember your own. Joseph Smith, reflecting on his own spiritual journey said: "If I had not experienced what I have, I would not believe it myself."[7] May we journey together in remembering our beliefs and rediscovering the Lord's hand in each of our lives.

---

[6] Ether 3:2-3, The Book of Mormon.
[7] Smith, Joseph. "Chapter 45: Joseph Smith's Feelings about His Prophetic Mission," *Teachings of Presidents of the Church: Joseph Smith*. 2007. Intellectual Reserve, Inc., Salt Lake City, 2011. https://www.churchofjesuschrist.org/study/manual/teachings-joseph-smith/chapter-45?lang=eng.

After the brother of Jared presents his stones to the Lord, we read this engaging passage, "...the Lord stretched forth his hand and touched the stones one by one with his finger. And the veil was taken from off the eyes of the brother of Jared..."[8]

As you read and ponder may your veil be lifted so you may see the Lord...

Let's look at another story where we can see once again a pattern the Lord uses as a reminder that he has not forgotten us. This next story is found in the Old Testament. We are in 1 Samuel, chapter 1. This is Hannah's story. In pondering Hannah, I am overcome with love and tenderness for her. As I read the few details of her life, I cannot help but feel a deep connection to her.

Perhaps you are familiar with Hannah? She is married to a righteous man named Elkanah. The scriptures tell us that Elkanah has two wives, Phinehas and Hannah. Phinehas has been blessed with children but Hannah has not been able to conceive a child. In fact, the scriptures teach us that because she was childless, Phinehas, "her adversary also provoked her sore."[9] Hannah's greatest desire was to have a son, but because her desire was not met her soul was conflicted. As I read the first passages of this account, I could imagine that Hannah felt forgotten.

It was the family's custom to travel to the temple each year to offer sacrifices. On one particular trip, like many they had made before, Hannah arose early and went to the grounds of the temple. There, she offered yet another heartfelt intentional plea for her righteous desire.

---

[8] Ether 3:6, The Book of Mormon.
[9] 1 Samuel 1:6, Holy Bible, KJV.

"And she was in bitterness of soul, and prayed unto the Lord, and wept sore. And she vowed a vow, and said O Lord of hosts, if thou wilt indeed look on the afflictions of thine handmaid, and remember me, and not forget thine handmaid."[10]

We are told in the verses that follow, "and the Lord remembered [Hannah]."[11] Hannah would return home, and conceive a son, who would become the Lord's chosen prophet.

My heart is touched when I read Hannah's story. I have felt that same "bitterness of soul"[12] and I have had times that I have "wept sore"[13] seeking for the Lord to "remember me"[14] in the midst of various trials. There have been moments, months, and miles I have walked when I have sought for understanding and comfort; times when I simply did not, or could not, understand why the desires of my heart were not met.

I believe that Hannah's story is one so many of us can relate to. We must not, we cannot forget the message of her story. Remember, we know how Hannah's story ends, we know "the Lord remembered her!"[15] Hannah's plea was heard; The Lord revealed his hand in her life! Hannah, overcome with gratitude, would dedicate her son to the Lord by offering him to Eli, the temple priest, to be raised as a servant of God in the Temple. This son, Samuel, would grow up to become the next prophet! Hannah would then be blessed to have five more children! Isn't this a beautiful story and pattern for how the Lord can show up in our lives?

---

[10] 1 Samuel 1:10-11, Holy Bible, KJV.
[11] 1 Samuel 1:19, Holy Bible, KJV.
[12] 1 Samuel 1:10, Holy Bible, KJV.
[13] Ibid.
[14] 1 Samuel 1:11, Holy Bible, KJV.
[15] 1 Samuel 1:19, Holy Bible, KJV.

I have learned over the years that Hannah's story is not isolated. Her story is only one example of what the Lord can do with our heartfelt pleas and even our tears.

> "*The Lord reveals himself to us, most often through the spirit, consistently and profoundly!*"
>
> - *Starr Anderson*

Let me take you to another remarkable story in the Bible that can help us see and understand how the Lord can appear to us. This time we are in the New Testament; John chapter 20. In 2019 the last chapters of John became two of my all-time favorite chapters in the scriptures, because of the personal message I found in their pages. These chapters have confirmed to me, again, that the Lord has a presence in our lives. He shows up when we are found "looking for him."

Let me begin by setting up the scene:

"The first day of the week cometh Mary Magdalene early, when it was yet dark, unto the sepulcher, and seeth the stone taken away from the sepulcher."[16]

These verses go on to tell us that, finding the sepulcher empty, Mary immediately runs to tell the disciples. Two of them return with her and indeed discover that the tomb is vacant.

---

[16] John 20:1, Holy Bible, KJV.

The account reads, "Then the disciples went away again unto their own home. But Mary stood without at the sepulcher weeping: and as she wept, she stooped down, and looked into the sepulcher."[17]

I cannot read these verses without my soul stirring. Mary had come to the tomb looking for the Savior. She had come to the place she believed he would be. She expected to find him. I have been like Mary! I have had moments when I have been searching for the Savior in my own life. I have gone to places that I was told he would be. I have read scriptures, attended meetings, and been to the temple. I have sought the Savior, and like Mary, there were times when I did not see him.

These verses have provided me with two powerful insights as I contemplate their imagery:

First, when Mary had verified the Lord was not in the tomb, she did not return home with the disciples. Instead, she STAYS at the tomb. Mary chooses to stay! Reading this the Spirit seems to ask me, "Are you willing to stay? When the answer does not come right away when the tomb seems so empty and you are unsure of what to do next, are you willing to stay? Are you willing to wait on the Lord?"

Second, Mary "looked into the sepulcher." Mary took an active role in her search. We will learn later that Mary will not recognize the Savior until she "turns" herself. These scriptures seem to be inviting me to change my focus and reevaluate my current direction. Turning involves action.

As Mary looks she "seeth two angels in white sitting...where the body of Jesus had lain. And they say unto her, 'Woman, why

---

[17] John 20:10-11, Holy Bible, KJV.

7

weepest thou?' She saith unto them, 'Because they have taken away my Lord, and *I know not*, where they have laid him.'"[18]

Have you ever heard yourself utter this plea? "I am looking for the Lord, I am looking for direction, but I cannot seem to find Him, I am unsure of what to do!"

"And when she had thus said, she turned herself back and saw Jesus standing, and knew not that it was Jesus. Jesus saith unto her, Woman why weepest thou? She, supposing him to be the gardener, saith unto him, Sir if thou have borne him hence, tell me where thou hast laid him, and I will take him away. Jesus saith unto her, 'Mary', she turned herself, and saith unto him, 'Rabboni'; which is to say Master."[19]

There are so many things I love about these verses. They can teach us how to recognize the Savior in our own lives and they remind us of a profound truth, the same truth was taught in Hannah's experience... The Lord shows up! He shows up! When we choose to stay, the Lord finds us!

Let me take a moment to point out a few more lessons we can learn from Mary's experience, and to perhaps reiterate a few things we have already looked at. First, go to where you believe and expect you should be able to find the Savior. Second, stay there! Third, take the time to look. Fourth, be willing to turn back. Fifth, sometimes the Savior is there but we are the ones who do not recognize him. Sixth, it's okay to weep! Seventh, we can tell the Lord who or what we are seeking. Eight, turn yourself (interesting that this same message has already been included in this verse. Perhaps we ought to again

---

[18] John 20:12-13, Holy Bible, KJV.
[19] John 20:14-16, Holy Bible, KJV.

8

ponder the importance of our effort to turn.) Finally, rely on the assurance that the Lord will and does come.

It is my belief that the scriptures can display powerful patterns for us and our own experiences can solidify the truths they teach.

Let me share with you a personal experience that has connected my heart to Mary and Hannah's experiences. My intent in sharing is that you might see your own unique experiences and how the Lord has manifested himself to YOU.

When I was a sophomore in college, I began to feel a desire to serve a mission. It was not something I had ever really planned on. My whole life I wanted to graduate from high school, meet the perfect guy, fall in love, get married, and have a family. When thoughts about serving a mission started coming I was actually very conflicted about my life's path. After some time, I expressed my concern to my Bishop who asked if he could give me a blessing. In that blessing, I was told that I was indeed being prepared to serve a mission. In time I received my mission call and went to the temple. I received a confirmation on one particular visit that I was not only called to serve a mission but that my mission call to Bilbao Spain was the exact place I needed to serve. I was excited. I left the Missionary Training Center knowing the Lord had called me to the work. I left for Spain with a rather firm conviction that I could single-handedly convert the entire country! That, of course, was before I knew the work was going to be hard. Really hard! In those long months, it seemed that no one wanted to listen, no matter how hard we prepared and worked. Then, after a few months out in the field, I woke up one morning to find that I had lost my hearing in one ear! I was at my breaking point.

I cried to Heavenly Father telling him that there had been a mistake. Somehow, I had misunderstood, I was not supposed to be a missionary. I felt lost, forsaken, and completely forgotten. I wrote home telling my family I surely did not have enough faith and the Lord really did not need me. I was ready to give up. It was almost two weeks before the next letter from home would arrive. It was from my father. My dad reminded me that "even prophets get sick and struggle with severe health issues." He reminded me that the Lord needed me and to rely on what I once knew to be true about my own call. He admonished me to take care of my health and like President Hinckley's father had once told him, "Forget yourself and go to work."[20]

I made a decision after reading my father's letter that I would double my efforts and do as he asked; I would get back to work. It would take a few weeks, but my hearing did return. The work continued to be hard. My companion(s) and I knocked doors, we did street contacts, we talked to members, and we sang songs in elevators. Still, few people listened.

After serving for about ten months, I was walking home one dark night with my companion, when I had an experience that has never left me. I was feeling rather beat up and wondering about the Lord's purpose and my part in his work. I remember gazing up into the night sky when I heard these words profound and clear in my mind, *"Starr, I know exactly where you are!"*

It would be a long thirteen months on my mission before I would see my first baptism! He was what other missionaries called a "golden"

[20] Hinckley, Gordon B. "Sweet Is the Work: Gordon B. Hinckley, 15th President of the Church." *New Era*, May 1995, www.churchofjesuschrist.org/study/new-era/1995/05/sweet-is-the-work-gordon-b-hinckley-15th-president-of-the-church?lang=eng.

investigator. Michael had traveled to Spain from Africa because of a stirring desire to seek the Lord's path for his own life. I did not know or understand until the week before I was headed home from Spain that the Lord had given him visions and dreams of the Book of Mormon. As a young boy, Michael had seen me in a dream. This dream reoccurred several times at pivotal points in his life. In his dream, he would see me and I would be carrying a blue book; the book he was told would lead him to God.

When I returned home from my mission, I was more beaten up than when I had left. I was trying to piece together my experience and wondering what the Lord was trying to teach me and what direction my life should be taking. It was a lonely time for me. I was full of

> *"The Lord shows up! He shows up! When we choose to stay, the Lord finds us!"*
> - Starr Anderson

questions and a desire to really know what the Lord would have me do. I found myself in Provo, Utah working fulltime and taking night classes at BYU.

One night as I finished my routine, I went to my small rented bedroom and opened my scriptures. I was reading in the Doctrine and Covenants when the phone rang. It was my weekly phone call from my Dad. After a small amount of chit-chat he finally said to me, "Starr, I want you to know that I am leaving the church. I have not believed for some time and I have found many resources to support my reasoning. I am calling to tell you first, because of all people, I figured you would understand. After serving a mission for eighteen months and only having one baptism, you would know and understand that the church simply cannot be true."

I do not recall the rest of that conversation. I do not know what I said or how the conversation ended. I remember hanging up the phone and just sitting there on that bed. I remember the tears that began to trickle. Here was my father, a good man, a man who raised our family in the gospel, who had written me faithfully on my mission, who had given me the advice I needed to keep going.... Here was my dad who no longer believed what he himself had taught me.

As I sat on that bed I looked over, and like Mary I found myself turning. There were my scriptures that I had tossed aside when the phone rang. I slowly picked them up and then I had another memory:

I think I must have been about 14-years-old, my mom had gone to the local church bookstore and bought scripture marking kits for my sisters and I. My mom was helping us work on a Personal Progress goal. We spent that summer sitting around the table and carefully coloring and labeling scriptures by topics. I had a beautiful set of scriptures. I remember it was that summer that I decided I really wanted to know for myself if the Book of Mormon was true. I had read the Book of Mormon, or at least most of it, so I decided one day I was going to pray about it.

My family lived on twenty acres out in the country in Central California. Behind our house, my dad had parked an old single-wide trailer. I remember going to that trailer and sitting on the bed in the back bedroom. I reread Moroni's promise and then I quietly knelt down to pray and ask God if what I had been learning about and reading about was really true. At the end of that bed in that old trailer, I received my first personal revelation or impression that the Book of Mormon in its entirety was indeed true. It was a feeling that filled me from head to toe. It planted in me a desire to want to continue to read and know more.

That is the memory that came to me as I sat on my bed in that little rented room, looking at my scriptures. The feeling I had felt in that old trailer, kneeling at the side of another bed, flooded back to me. I knew I had a choice to make that night. Either my dad was right about the church not being true or the feeling I had experienced as a young girl was a manifestation of the Spirit and the Book of Mormon was in fact true! As I prayed that night for more direction my mind was filled with memories of my mission and specifically the night I heard the Lord speak to me, "Starr, I know exactly where you are." Like Mary, although I had not really felt the impact of her story back then, I was making a choice to stay.

Somehow I found the courage to call my dad back on the phone. It was the first time I would openly oppose him in a conversation. I remember saying to him something along the lines of, "Dad, I am sorry, but you are wrong. The gospel is true. I know the Book of Mormon is true, and I know that God is aware of me!" The spirit filled my heart as I verbally communicated my testimony.

That particular experience was a pivotal point in my life. That experience, sitting on a tiny bed in a basement apartment was a reminder to me of how often the Lord had shown up in my life. He had shown up in a single-wide trailer, he had shown up on the streets of Spain, and He showed up again to remind me of what I had already experienced. The Lord does not leave us alone!

I share this with you because I am no different than you. I have felt what the people of King Benjamin describe when "they viewed themselves in their own carnal state, even less than the dust of the earth."[21] However, in the midst of all my inadequacies the Lord has still shown up in my life. The Lord has spoken to my heart and my

---

[21] Mosiah 4:1-3, The Book of Mormon

prayers have been answered. I have come to understand that if the Lord can remember me, He can and will remember you!

Can I take you back to the book of John? We are in chapter 20 again. I want to include a few more verses from this chapter because I know there are readers thinking, "but not me, this has not been my experience! I have not felt the same promptings or had answers come so easily." There are those who can relate, perhaps more easily, to the Lord's disciple, Thomas.

We often refer to Thomas as "Doubting Thomas." We learn that after Mary's experience at the tomb, that evening the disciples were gathered together. Then "came Jesus and stood in the midst, and saith unto them, Peace be unto you."[22] What a glorious experience for the disciples to see the resurrected Savior and to feel his hand and see the prints in his feet. "Then were the disciples glad, when they saw the Lord."[23]

"But Thomas, one of the twelve, called Didymus, was not with them when Jesus came."[24]

I have pondered these verses over and over and my heart simply aches for Thomas. Where was Thomas? Why of all experiences did he have to miss this one? Was Thomas out ministering or visiting a sick ward member? Was Thomas alone somewhere in prayer? Perhaps he was just busy completing regular, mundane, daily tasks. Or, was he doing something perhaps that he shouldn't have been doing? In pondering these things I see myself in Thomas. Sometimes my experience is not the same as others. Sometimes I have felt that I "missed" it and that I have simply been left out and forgotten! In my

---

[22] John 20:19, Holy Bible, KJV.
[23] John 20:20, Holy Bible, KJV.
[24] John 20:24, Holy Bible, KJV.

mind, I see beloved Thomas, who early on in Christ's ministry, was quick to defend and stand in allegiance. My heart feels Thomas' pain. The Savior has come and gone, and he has missed it!

Can we not hear ourselves in Thomas' famous cry, "except I shall see in his hands the prints of the nails and put my finger into the prints of the nails, and thrust my hand into his side, I will not believe"[25]? Have you ever uttered a similar cry? I wish it was not so, but I have. I have wanted proof, I have wanted assurance, I have wanted an experience....

Hidden in verse 28 are three profound lessons Thomas can teach us.

"And after eight days, again his disciples were within, and Thomas with them, then came Jesus, the doors being shut, and stood in their midst, and said, Peace be unto you."[26]

Can you see the insights and lessons in this simple verse? I want to point out a few of them. First, Thomas stays with the disciples. Even though Thomas has not had the same experience, he chooses to stay. He stays with the believers despite feeling left out. Did we not just see this pattern in John's account of Mary? We, too, can choose to stay. When our experience has not been the same as others, we can stay with those who will share their testimony and experience with us. Second, when we have had an experience, we must allow other people to be with us. We should invite others to be with us. Let us gather, accept, teach, and provide a place of safety for those who are willing and trying to wait on the Lord. Third, again, a pattern from Mary's experience... the Lord does come! The Lord will show up! I am happy for Thomas that it was only eight days later that the Lord again appears. But I hope that if it is eight days, eight weeks, eight

---

[25] John 20:25, Holy Bible, KJV.
[26] John 20:26, Holy Bible, KJV.

months, or eight years… the Lord will find me waiting! Remember, Nephi's family was in the wilderness for eight years before they built the ship that would lead them to the promised land.

Don't you just love Thomas? Please Stay. Please Wait. Please be found with the believers.

> *"He sent His Son, even our Savior, Jesus Christ, who is capable of finding each and every one of us."*
> - Starr Anderson

Let's go ahead and finish John's account in the Bible. After all, it has a few more intriguing lessons. It contains more beautiful truths about how and when the Savior shows up, and perhaps has a little more insight on what we can do when we are feeling lost and forgotten.

John 21 is a part of Peter's story. Again, this is a story so many of you are familiar with:

The resurrected Savior has left the disciples.

"There were together Simon Peter, and Thomas called Didymus, and Nathanael of Cana in Galilee, and the sons of Zebedee, and two other of His disciples. Simon Peter saith unto them, I go a fishing. They say unto him, We also go with thee. They went forth and entered into a ship immediately; and that night they caught nothing."[27]

Now I want to take a minute and set up the framework for this story. As a young girl, whenever I heard this Bible story I often heard

---

[27] John 21:2-3, Holy Bible, KJV.

16

comments about why Peter returned to fishing. "Fishing is what Peter knew. He was returning to his old way of life. Without the Savior's guidance Peter probably felt lost." Perhaps there is some truth to these thoughts and comments. But, recently as I studied and pondered this account, something came to my mind. I saw Peter, beautiful faithful Peter, being called as a disciple. Peter's first recorded experience with the Savior was while he was on a fishing boat, "And Jesus, walking by the sea of Galilee, saw two brethren, Simon called Peter, and Andrew his brother, casting a net into the sea: for they were fishers. And he saith unto them, Follow me, and I will make you fishers of men."[28] I cannot help but wonder if Peter, uncertain of what to do now that the Savior had left again, felt a little lost. Could it be that Peter returned to the very thing he was doing when the Savior *first* came to him?... Fishing! To me this is a beautiful thought; one I can relate to. It is an action that is full of faith. Peter is setting for us an example of what to do when we are lost or unsure...we can go back to what we once knew. We can return to times and places when we have seen and felt the Savior's influence in our lives!

As a teenager, I often felt the Savior's love for me as I lay on our trampoline in the backyard. I would wait until it was dark, just as the stars would be appearing and I would go outside to lay on the trampoline and look at the vast universe and ponder. It was on dark starry nights that I often felt stillness, peace, and what I believe is the influence of the Holy Ghost. In writing this now, it is clear to me why the Lord spoke to me at night while walking the streets of Spain, "*Starr, I know exactly where you are.*" He knew I was familiar with the night sky and knew that is where I would recognize His voice.

---

[28] Matthew 4:18-19, Holy Bible, KJV.

We all have fishing boats. When we are lost there are places we can return to. Your list might include the sky, places out in nature, your car, the temple, church, your closet, the side of your bed, or your scriptures. Is your ship in the harbor waiting for you?

I don't want to move on until I point out one more insight from this verse about Peter's declaration to go fishing. A few months ago, I found myself struggling. I was seeking personal direction, yet once again... I had just been released from a calling I had held for almost 7 years. I could not seem to find purpose. I was sitting at my desk rereading this account in the scriptures and I sent my husband the following text: "I'm going fishing!" Unaware of my emotional meltdown, or the connection I was making with this particular scripture, his immediate reply was, "uh, okay?" followed by, "can I go with you?" I sat there at my desk crying. I understood a little of how Peter must have felt when he declared his intent to return to his ship, and his beloved friends, I imagine, boldly declared "we go with thee!"

I want to be like those disciples! When others are seeking I want to be a part of their journey! I want to be someone they can count on. I want my response to be a quick, "I'm coming with you!"

"But when the morning was now come, Jesus stood on the shore: but the disciples knew not that it was Jesus. And he said unto them, Cast the net on the right side of the ship, and ye shall find. They cast therefore, and now they were not able to draw if for the multitude of fishes. Therefore that disciple whom Jesus loved saith unto Peter, It is the Lord. Now when Simon Peter heard that it was the Lord, he girt his fisher's coat unto him, and did cast himself into the sea."[29]

---

[29] John 21:4-7, Holy Bible, KJV.

I want to point out three lessons that we can learn from this one verse. First, the Lord has appeared, but the disciples do not recognize him at first. Can you see the parallel with Mary's account? This causes me to ponder how often the Lord shows up in my life and I do not know or understand that He is right there! Second, I love that it is John that exclaims and points out to Peter that the Savior is on the shore. I want to be a John. I want to be directing others to the Savior. I want to help them see as they return to their boats with hope. Third, the Lord shows up. Again, we continue to see this familiar pattern. When we go seeking the Lord... He does come! Not only does the Lord fill our nets, but He shows Himself unto us.

I want to be a fisherwoman!

Before I conclude, I want you to know that by declaring testimony of the assurance that God shows up in our lives, it does not mean our lives will be without trouble or difficulty. In fact, like many prophets of old, I have learned for myself that it is often in the very midst of our trials that the Lord reveals his hand and comes to comfort our hearts. Let me share one last personal experience:

One of my most cherished encounters with the Lord happened in April of 2003. I had received the news that my mother, who had recently turned fifty, was in the hospital after suffering a stroke. The doctors informed us that she had experienced what they called "a bleeder." This stroke caused rapid damage and required immediate brain surgery. As soon as I could, I flew from my home in Utah to California to be with my mother. I took my six-month-old daughter with me and left my two-year-old daughter behind with my husband. It was a long week to be at my mom's side watching her lose part of her speech and movement. It was a time of contemplation and a time of hope. My father, my siblings, and I prayed. We begged and pleaded for my mother to recover. On one occasion my uncle came to give my mom a blessing. In that blessing, he said she would make a full recovery. In the very moment he uttered those words, however, something piercing told me she would not make a full recovery. Moments later in the hallway my uncle looked at me and said, "I am so sorry, that is what I wanted!" I knew he had also felt what I had felt. I could not fault my uncle, the brother who had been a constant in her life, for verbalizing the profound desire that we all shared. Those thoughts had simply escaped his lips during that blessing. The spirit had instantly corrected his words, and we both knew it.

I returned to my home soon after, I needed to get back to my daughter and husband. I left knowing my mom would remain paralyzed. It would be almost two weeks before I would get the phone call from my father that would change the course of my life... my mother had passed away.

Where was God in this moment? When the darkness and the reality started to hit that my beautiful mother was gone, where was the Lord? I will tell you where He was, He was right there! I remember laying on the tiled kitchen floor in the fetal position sobbing, a sob I have yet to experience again. It hurt. It was painful. The Lord did not take the pain away but somehow in the midst of it, I felt a stillness, a peace. It was a peace I had not yet felt so profoundly in my life. It was real. It was powerful. The Lord had shown up when I needed Him the very most.

I boldly echo the words of Alma, "...give ear to my words; for I swear unto you, that inasmuch as ye shall keep the commandments of God ye shall prosper in the land. I would that you should do as I have done, in remembering the captivity of our fathers; for they were in bondage, and none could deliver them except it was the God of Abraham, and the God of Isaac, and the God of Jacob; and he surely delivered them in their afflictions...I beseech of thee that thou wilt hear my words and learn of me; for I do know that whosoever shall put their trust in God shall be supported in their trials, and their troubles, and their afflictions..."[30]

God, our Heavenly Father, has not forsaken us! Instead, He sent His Son, even our Savior, Jesus Christ, who is capable of finding each and every one of us. We must seek Him. He will find us. May we search for Him. Let us continue to plead with the Lord to remember us. Let us choose to stay. Let us gather with the disciples. Let us "go fishing". Let us wait in our wildernesses. Let us trust that the Lord will come! Let us put forth our effort as we present our stones for Him to touch. Let us turn and behold Him. And then, let us unite in our declaration that we have been found! This is my prayer, this is my hope.

---

[30] Alma 36:1-3, The Book of Mormon.

God, our Heavenly Father,
has not forsaken us!
Instead, He sent His Son,
even our Savior, Jesus Christ,
who is capable of finding each
and every one of us.

- Starr Anderson -

—— 2 ——
Chelsea Bowen Bretzke
More Sense of Their Care

I lay on my yoga mat, so sore from three long days of straight driving. My closed eyelids are like a thin veil against the brightness of the almost thick feeling sunlight. "There are so many birds," I think as I listen to their varied chirps and calls. It's so green. So alive. It seems so unfamiliar after what feels like the longest winter of my life, full of times when my spirit felt anything but alive.

We have unexpectedly relocated our family from our home in Canada to the Southern United States. My husband and I, and our seven children; our oldest with special needs and our youngest, five months, and still nursing. All this during the worldwide COVID-19 pandemic. I should be completely overwhelmed by it all. At times I am. But as I lay here surrounded by extraordinarily tall trees in our incredibly lush temporary backyard, I hear Him.

A moment of knowing. A message felt and received. A knowing outside of words. But if I had to translate, it feels like God saying:

> "I know.
> I know what you need.
> I know what you have endured.
> I know what is yet to come.
> I'm giving you *this*.
> This time.
> This place.
> This "garden" of sorts—
> To heal
> To listen
> To be with Me."

All that and more is communicated with a swirl of the Spirit: an essence, an invitation. Summed up? *"Come, child, come."*

Even as I am given this tender message, I resist. I feel dumb. I trivialize myself and my experiences. Why do I need to heal? There are so many worse things people have suffered: traumas, abuse, violence, illness. And in many ways, I feel that I have created my pain or at least chosen it. And somehow, I think that means I should suffer. But hurt people hurt people, so that means my kids suffer, too, and I don't want that. I don't want them raised by a mom who is such a wild card—loving and fun one day—harsh and irritable the next. I also want them to love themselves—more than anything I want them to love themselves! And I know so profoundly the only way to lead them to that is not by telling them, but by showing them, giving them a model of it by my own soul's journey. I want to show them that they can't love God (really) and loathe themselves (as I have been so prone to do). That gives me the desire to believe that I need to stop resisting and start believing the Spirit's message. And while I lay here, love—not just the generic "God loves all His children" kind of love, but a specific, intensely intimate and personal love, *just for me*, nudges me over the edge and convinces me to accept the invitation.

Responding to the invitation.

What follows feels like the condensed university class I took once during the spring semester, every day jam-packed with learning. But it's also strangely slow, unfrenzied, filled with drawn-out sessions of contemplating and feeling. I observe a bug, a bird, my baby, my body. My children clamor, but they, too, are happily exploring our new surroundings. Miraculously, I feel their needs softly muted, still there, still needing attending to, but not as demanding. I feel drawn to draw and write poetry, both things I hadn't done in years. It's a desire to conceptualize things I'm thinking about into images that evoke feelings I can't fully explain. I walk, with the baby in her carrier nestled hot against me in the thick humidity. I do yoga with toddlers crawling under my downward dogs. And I just lay in the grass on my dingy old yoga mat, letting my mind float with the clouds overhead.

Many of these things I have done all my adult life. But *this* time, there is a lingering sense that God is with me, guiding me towards the next lesson. I fill my journal with hopelessly inadequate descriptions of the things I feel my soul is learning: about God, about the world, about my family, but also, about myself. Author Sue Monk Kidd has written, "In some ways, spiritual development for women, perhaps unlike that for men, is not about surrendering self so much as coming to self."[31] This idea resonates so deeply with

---

[31] Kidd, Sue Monk. *The Dance of the Dissonant Daughter.* (1996) HarperCollins Publishers, 2016, p.107.

my soul. Rather than striving to decrease or become somehow smaller, I feel that as my Heavenly Parents draw me closer to Them, I feel an increase, an addition of light and truth, a clearer vision and even magnification of my own inherited divinity. An exciting discovery and enlarging of my soul. Coming to God, experiencing such infinite, powerful love, allows us to come more fully to ourselves. To feel more at home within. To become more whole. God isn't just saying, "I love you," He's saying you *are lovable.* He wants each of us to see our lovability through His eyes, and most importantly to *feel* that love in all that we do. Former Relief Society general president, Bonnie D. Parkin, often repeated such a vision, "If I could have one thing happen for every woman in this Church, it would be that they would feel the love of the Lord in their lives daily."[32] She continues, "I have felt the love of the Lord in my life, and I am so thankful for that."[33] Oh, how thankful I also am for God's incredible love. They—Father, Mother—nurtured me in my 'garden' in a way I haven't quite experienced before; at least in such concentration. Yet, as I think about what this experience taught me about God's ability to nurture us, I've come to realize that it is indeed a constant process. A process that, if we choose to become aware of, would help us feel the unfathomable love and support Heaven *always* has to offer.

A familiar feeling.

This daily, nurturing love invites us to grow and reminds us we experienced its power long before this life. President Dallin H. Oaks recently taught, "As spirits, we desired to achieve the eternal life enjoyed by our heavenly parents. At that point, we had progressed as far as we could."[34] Even more clearly he proclaimed: "The purpose of mortal life and the mission of The Church of Jesus Christ of

---

[32] Parkin, Bonnie D. "Feel the Love of the Lord," Liahona, July 2002, pg.95; Ensign, May 2002, pg.84
[33] Ibid.

Latter-day Saints is to prepare the sons and daughters of God for their eternal destinies--to become like our heavenly parents."[35] Of such doctrine, Sister Sharon Eubank has testified: "Knowing this truth helps me understand my eternal purpose. I came to the earth with eons of experience and talent. I also came with certain responsibilities personal to me."[36] The idea of eons of nurturing, unique to our faith, is an empowering thought to me. The time we spent learning in the premortal realm makes our earthly learning feel less like random predestination and much more of a continued opportunity for growth. This context also leaves room for both our righteous desires and our ever-developing testimonies of Christ to have begun long before our physical births.

I love the image another woman once shared with me where she imagined counseling with her Heavenly Parents as they discussed her hopes and plans for earth life. "What would you like to accomplish?", they might have asked. "What are you interested in learning? doing? contributing through your unique gifts you have developed so far? What do you think will be difficult, or in what areas do you still feel that you need to develop more in order to be more like us? What do you need to learn to be prepared for additional, future glories?"

I like thinking we participated in some of the decisions concerning what our experience on earth would be like, and that our Heavenly Parents continue to strive to engage us in our training as apprentice creators. This intuitive image of this personal farewell was doctrinally confirmed when I read the teachings of President Harold B. Lee who wrote:

---

[34] Oaks, Dallin H. "The Great Plan," General Conference April 2020
[35] Oaks, Dallin H. "Same-Gender Attraction," *Ensign*, October 1995, https://www.churchofjesuschrist.org/study/ensign/1995/10/same-gender-attraction?lang=eng
[36] Eubank, Sharon. "A Letter to a Single Sister." *Ensign*, Oct. 2019, www.churchofjesuschrist.org/study/ensign/2019/10/a-letter-to-a-single-sister?lang=eng.

"There came a day, then, when Mother and Father said, 'Now, my son, my daughter, it is now your time to go."[37] He continued, "We forget that we have a Heavenly Father and a Heavenly Mother who are even more concerned, probably, than our earthly father and mother, and that influences from beyond are constantly working to try to help..."[38] More recently Jean B. Bingham reminded us we are eternal beings, the literal offspring of God and added, "What a glorious spirit-hood we must have had in that premortal time!"[39] She reiterated that our divine worth is absolute because of our divine parentage. "Your Heavenly Parents prepared you to come to earth with those truths embedded in your spirit."[40] She taught we were excited to try to become like Them because "We saw Their happiness and instinctively wanted that same joy."[41]

Elder Jeffrey R. Holland and his wife, Patricia, have taught that our Mother and our Father are involved in the ongoing process of creating everything around us, and "are doing so lovingly and carefully and masterfully."[42]

As the ultimate parents, our Heavenly Parents are master nurturers. To nurture means to care for and encourage the growth or development of someone or something.[43] Once we know and understand how much our Heavenly Parents want to, *and do*, nurture us then it's up to us to accept it. How do we accept the nurturing care of our loving Heavenly Parents? I find myself constantly going back

[37] Lee, Harold B. "The Influence and Responsibility of Women," *Relief Society Magazine* 51, Intellectual Reserve, Inc., February 1964, p.85.
[38] Ibid.
[39] Bingham, Jean B. "How to Be Happy Now-and Forever." *BYU Speeches*, 10 Dec. 2019, speeches.byu.edu/talks/jean-b-bingham/how-happy-now-forever/.
[40] Ibid. Doctrine and Covenants 138:56
[41] Ibid.
[42] Holland, Patricia T. "Filling the Measure of Our Creation," in Jeffrey R. Holland and Patricia T. Holland, *On Earth As It Is in Heaven*, Deseret Book Company, Salt Lake City, 1989, p.4.
[43] *Nurture: Definition of Nurture by Oxford Dictionary on Lexico.com Also Meaning of Nurture.* 2020, www.lexico.com/en/definition/nurture.

to the foundational truth taught by the prophet Joseph Smith, "It is the first principle of the gospel to know for a certainty the character of God."[44] He pleads with the Saints, "I want you all to know Him and to be familiar with Him."[45] But to do so, he said, we must have "a correct idea of his ... perfections, and attributes," an admiration for "the excellency of [His] character."[46]

Let's explore God's nurturing character; how he cares for and encourages our individual growth.

God will never force.

I admit, my mothering heart hasn't always loved the word nurture. In the past, my mind has conjured up images of thriving plants and well-behaved children, and the poised, seemingly perfect woman smiling humbly behind them—the source of it all. That results-driven view infuriated me because none of the little humans I was "growing" seemed to want any of my input, and I couldn't keep a plant alive to save my life! I also didn't really want the praise these "perfect" women received, because then I'd have to take the blame if things didn't turn out to a picture-perfect standard. Yet ultimately, at the heart of my resistance was an unwillingness to believe any individual soul should be controlled by another.

"Our right to choose is eternal,"[47] taught Sister Chieko N. Okazaki, adding that "We sometimes teach that it is God-given but even that is not completely accurate, it is God-protected, but the right to

---

[44] Smith, Joseph. as referenced by Jeffrey R. Holland, "The Grandeur of God." *Ensign*, Nov. 2003, www.churchofjesuschrist.org/study/ensign/2003/11/the-grandeur-of-god?lang=eng.
[45] Ibid.
[46] Ibid.
[47] Okazaki, Chieko N. *Being Enough.* Bookcraft Inc., Salt Lake City, 2002, p.168.

choose is part of our eternal being. God cannot and will not take that right away from us..."[48]

> "*The time we spent learning in the premortal realm makes our earthly learning feel less like random predestination and much more of a continued opportunity for growth.*"
>
> *- Chelsea Bretzke*

An often-heard phrase in our house is "Don't force!" With seven kids, they are all eager to have their moments as the "big" kid, to be the one "in charge." Even their sincere attempts to help can quickly morph into a battle of wills, clenched teeth, and "Do it this way!" After a few family scripture studies focused on the eternal principle of choice within the plan of salvation (and hopefully as a result applied more in our home), my daughter would often remind her older brother, "Don't be Satan!" when he tried to make her do something she didn't want to do. We've tried to rephrase that to a request for more Jesus inspired interaction, instead of calling our siblings the devil. Such honoring of choice plays out in such small things: asking a toddler do you want the blue shirt or the rainbow one? Do you want to try and do up your seatbelt or do you want me to help? (that one can backfire in a time crunch!) It makes such a difference to their little spirits to grow their autonomy.

And it only gets more crucial as they get older. After all, as Elder Dale G. Renlund taught, "Our Heavenly Father's goal in parenting is not to have His children do what is right; it is to have His children *choose* to do what is right."[49] If our goal is to parent like Them, no

[48] Ibid.
[49] Renlund, Dale G. "Choose You This Day," General Conference October 2018

amount of coercion, manipulation, or any form of ultimatums is ever appropriate. Spiritual things cannot be forced. Repentance, testimony, and desire are all precious fruits of what happens inside our individual souls. Luckily, God has a plan to grow all those things in the hearts of our children, and us.

His plan to nurture us is as individual as we are.

My oldest son, Aaron, has autism and is almost completely non-verbal. Throughout elementary school, he was in an inclusive program, where he was in a regular classroom with his neurotypical peers, but with a full-time aid and a personalized learning plan. A lot of time and effort went into trying to come up with meaningful goals that would help him, however slowly, progress. It would have been ridiculous to expect him to learn and do at the same level as the other students in his class. His specific needs required a specific, drastically adapted approach. I believe good teachers implement some sort of individuality to all of their teachings, and God is the ultimate teacher. Yet sometimes, we start to think the gospel is a one size fits all program. Because the principles are so eternal, we forget that God has individual plans for us as well, based on gospel truths.

Sister Sharon Eubank shares how our "macro-mission"[50] in essence is like everyone's: to "have experiences, repent and forgive, gain ordinances, serve others."[51] But then she expounds, "My micro-mission, however, is specific and part of a divine plan for me."[52] She reassures us that if we're doing our best to keep our covenants, the life we're living now is part of that plan. Do you believe that God has a micro-mission for you? Do you trust that our Heavenly Parents know you well enough to have a customized curriculum, at your own

---

[50] Eubank, Sharon. "A Letter to a Single Sister." *Ensign*, Oct. 2019, www.churchofjesuschrist.org/study/ensign/2019/10/a-letter-to-a-single-sister?lang=eng.
[51] Ibid.
[52] Ibid.

pace, designed for your optimal growth and development? A plan just for you? Their child. A child They know better than you even know yourself?

Years ago I felt an impression to go through the Book of Mormon with our then, very young sons. We tied neckties around their little foreheads, made tin foil gold-plates, and toilet paper roll iron rods. I made a particularly striking "wicked king Noah" headdress out of construction paper. We have used our little yarn craft-fur beard for everything from Lehi to Jesus, for years now. As I posted our fun on social media, the only consistent family documentation I seem to be able to manage, people frequently asked me to share my lesson plans. It wasn't that I was against sharing them, if I'd felt inspired to I would have. But what I thought every time someone asked me was, "But this is what *I* felt inspired to do with *my* kids!" Sure, we were loosely working our way through the Book of Mormon, but whether I emphasized Nephi's obedience, or forgiveness, Alma's conversion or missionary service, Moroni's brave rallying or lonely endurance was dependent on what was happening that particular week in our home and the little hearts of my sons. Even at that young age, when they basically knew nothing of the gospel, I still trusted that God had certain concepts He wanted to be taught. He knew the most effective way to get it into their individual souls—whether that was building King Benjamin Lego towers, or throwing paper-ball stones at a prophet standing on the back of the couch. Even now, with older and more kids, I still feel that way.

President Russell M. Nelson has not stressed us hearing Him[53] because it makes a catchy hashtag. His task, as the prophet of God, is to teach an *entire* world how to come unto Christ. Within the church alone, we are an ever-expanding and ever-diversifying group. As

---

[53] Nelson, Russell M. "Hear Him," General Conference April 2020

general authorities, they teach general principles, true doctrine that is then our job to apply.

Elder David A. Bednar has explained that it is not the responsibility of the Church to do and teach us everything we think we need to know to be better disciples and endure to the end. He clarifies, "our personal responsibility is to learn what we should learn, to live as we know we should live, and to become who the Master would have us become."[54] How can we do that if we do not learn how to listen to Heavenly guidance instructing us on how to do so?

For me, this means effort. As our prophet has declared, "The Lord loves effort."[55] But also excitement! It means I must put in the energy to uncover the things God wants me to learn. It means time in the scriptures and on my knees, and sometimes lying on a yoga mat under a tree, trying to hear Him. It means speaking and listening to others, especially other women, hearing what they have learned. It's reading books, listening to podcasts and gathering thoughts and ideas and trusting God to lead me to *my* next thing (even a family movie can convey priceless truths!) It means that God really does have a plan specific to me and I get to discover what it is!

Trusting God to give us the next nourishing piece.

As we trust in God's individual plan for our individual learning, we will come to recognize His curriculum is cumulative and customized. As Ardeth G. Kapp expounded upon the well-known scriptural phrase, "Glimpses of understanding come line upon line, precept upon precept. Our Father is anxious to feed us just as fast as we can handle it, but we regulate the richness and the volume of our

---

[54] Bednar, David A. "Prepared to Obtain Every Needful Thing," General Conference April 2019

[55] Nelson, Russell M. as cited in "An Especially Noble Calling," General Conference April 2020

spiritual diet."[56] In my own experience nurturing my large family, there is always another hungry tummy, a mouth wanting more.

In his talk, "To Acquire Spiritual Guidance,"[57] Elder Richard G. Scott tells of an experience where he received an outpouring of personal revelation. He carefully recorded and pondered what he had received, thanking the Lord for it. Then twice he asked, "Is there more I should know?"[58] And both times more came and he "received some of the most precious, specific, personal direction one could hope to obtain in this life."[59] He carefully emphasized the importance of cherishing the initial inspiration and then asking if there is more. When I have followed this pattern, I have come to learn God is always ready with the next piece and that blessings can be predicated upon our request. We need to ask the next question and then wait for the next bit of light.[60] Joy D. Jones has encouraged us that once we have offered up the desires of our hearts to God, we then "focus on His light guiding our life choices and resting upon us when we turn to Him"[61] realizing that "He knows each of us by name and has individual roles for us to fulfill."[62] It's our own little path of breadcrumbs. Or to be more scriptural—our daily manna— the heavenly provided nourishment for our souls. It's the oil that accrues drop by drop but is also burning in our spiritual lamps and thus needs constant adding to. So, I seek the next piece of my puzzle. The next phase of my journey. The next insight that will set my heart aflame. It doesn't mean there aren't times we don't feel lost; where the trail goes cold and I scream at the heavens to help me find a way from the encroaching darkness. But when the light comes, and the next piece falls into place? There is an absolute thrill to it.

---

[56] Kapp, Ardeth G. "Drifting, Dreaming, Directing," *At the Pulpit: 185 Years of Discourses by Latter-day Saint Women*. Intellectual Reserve, Inc.,2017, p.195.
[57] Scott, Richard G. "To Acquire Spiritual Guidance," General Conference October 2009
[58] Ibid.
[59] Ibid.
[60] Doctrine and Covenants 50:24
[61] Jones, Joy D. "An Especially Noble Calling," General Conference April 2020
[62] Ibid.

Once you've tasted the pure nourishment of heaven, other lesser things tend to lose their savor and are not nearly as satisfying. Eliza R. Snow taught, "Saints of God can be edified by nothing but the Spirit of God."[63] She explained that we had "attained to an elevation so high ...that nothing but the revelations of heaven would edify [us]."[64] Those edifying experiences have been customized for each of us: an individualized stringing together of tender mercies into a relationship of trust, love of the Lord every day that's delivered in specific ways to help us identify it. I have come to realize that receiving from the Spirit (to me) is a very energizing process. Praying while I walk, run, or even drive helps me focus on what the Lord wants to teach me. The church's youth theme albums, as well as other Christian praise music, helps get my spirit fired-up; a spiritual warm-up preparing me to open my heart to receive what God has in store. Tender mercy moments have come countless times as the random conference talk I cue up on my run brings me to tears as it addresses the very questions or concerns I had been contemplating. It has been almost comical the extent to which the Lord has gone to convince me of His awareness and involvement.

Certain books I felt prompted to pack for our move, that I've owned for years, I would randomly open to chapters that expounded upon the exact gospel topics or symbols I was studying. Halfway through the summer, we moved to another short-term rental. It was hard leaving my "garden" where I had spent so much time with God. Yet He had other gifts to bestow, including an old slightly out of tune piano and a firepit, knowing both would be particularly soothing to my soul. I haven't always recognized God's generosity to me. In fact, I'm still learning to trust God as the ultimate giver of good gifts.[65]

---

[63] Snow, Eliza R. "An Elevation so High Above the Ordinary," *At the Pulpit: 185 Years of Discourses by Latter-day Saint Women.* Intellectual Reserve, Inc.,2017, p.56.
[64] Ibid.
[65] St. Matthew 11:7, Holy Bible, KJV.

Growing up, despite my parents' best efforts, I learned to expect disappointment when it came to gifts. With our economic situation I never seemed to get what I really wanted. And so I gave up. At times I have projected that self-learned denial upon God, viewing Him as the one asking me to give up the things I want. An erroneous conclusion that what I desired and what God desired for me were diametrically opposed. But as someone recently pointed out, "You're overlooking one thing Chelsea, your desires are good!" God's tender, personal, sweet gifts to me are teaching me not only how well He knows my heart and all its good desires but reassuring me that He wants those good things for me too. Elder David A. Bednar testified "that the tender mercies of the Lord are real and that they do not occur randomly or merely by coincidence."[66] He further taught "that the Lord's tender mercies are the very personal and individualized blessings, strength, protection, assurances, guidance, loving-kindnesses, consolation, support, and spiritual gifts which we receive from, because of, and through the Lord Jesus Christ."[67] Tender mercies are the punctuation of the Lord's curriculum for each of us. This is not just an intellectual endeavor. He wants to change our very hearts. To do so, He must convince us of His care. Like a string of pearls, or the consecutive clues to our scavenger hunt, when placed together, the individual threads of each tender mercy moment weave together a tapestry that tells a story of profound involvement and an intimate knowing that convinces us that we are known, not just as we are now, but as we can become. Sister Sheri L. Dew taught it is the "Spirit who reveals to us our identity—which isn't just who we are but who we have always been."[68] She went on to say that when we know, "our lives take on a sense of purpose so stunning that we can never be the same again."[69]

---

[66] Bednar, David A. "The Tender Mercies of the Lord," General Conference April 2005
[67] Ibid.
[68] Dew, Sheri L. "Knowing Who You Are-and Who You Have Always Been." *The Church Historian's Press*, 19 Apr. 2016, www.churchhistorianspress.org/at-the-pulpit/part-4/Chapter-48?lang=eng.
[69] Ibid.

We are known and we are meant to fly!

To reach the divine potential within each of us, almost even more than effort, I have come to realize the need for trust. Trust that God knows me so, so well. That He knows all the jumble of thoughts and all the complex feelings those thoughts create. It means I trust Him to give me exactly what will help me take my next steps forward, to add more light to my understanding.

He guides me to the cliff edges of my current comprehension, and asks, "Do you trust me?" We all have our times when we pull our figurative pioneer handcarts and like those early church pioneers, faithfully move forward to unknown destinations. In these often duty propelled times, our trudging may be to prove to our God and ourselves that whatever He requires we will give, with bloody feet, and shallow graves. But I have also come to know a God who invites us to take His hand and fly. A God who has heights and depths, mountain tops with celestial views, pillars of light for us to inhabit and explore—faces to the sky, hearts burning, eyes transfigured.

> *"Once you've tasted the pure nourishment of heaven, other lesser things tend to lose their savor and are not nearly as satisfying."*
>
> - *Chelsea Bretzke*

Yet sometimes we just keep walking, heads down, plodding on our known, comfortable path. A good path. A dutiful path. A path that will eventually lead to eternal life. But we ignore the current joy and life He would breathe into us, willingly. Pushing beyond our current spiritual understandings, abilities, and identity is one of the most joyful, life-invigorating endeavors we could ever pursue. So why wouldn't we stay engaged in such a journey? I think sometimes there is fear that maybe there isn't much more of our spiritual potential to discover. Maybe we aren't that special. Truman G. Madsen, in response to the idea we all feel at times that we, "don't amount to much,"[70] we are not "one of those good ones,"[71] or, as a student said to him, "I think I'm just basically telestial material."[72] In response, he testified that "...even the person you think the worst of"[73] which he added can often be ourselves, "the truth is that the embryo within the worst of us is divine. The truth is that there is nothing you can do to really destroy that fact. The potential is there."[74]

God knows that potential is nurtured best by experience.

I have always loved the quote by Orson F. Whitney that shares how none of the pains or trials we experience are wasted. That it "ministers to our education"[75] contributing to our overall learning, growth, and development. It is so comforting to know all our suffering when endured with the Lord's help "builds up our characters, purifies our hearts, expands our souls"[76] making us more "tender and charitable."[77] To realize and remember our hard things are helping us become all we need to be, and that it is through our hard, even painful experiences "that we gain the education that we come here to acquire and which will make us more like our Father and Mother in heaven."[78]

I've learned sorrow and suffering alone do not lead us to Christ. Many have suffered greatly, and it leads only to bitterness and hate.

---

[70] Madsen, Truman G. "The Highest in Us." *BYU Speeches*, 4 Feb. 2020, speeches.byu.edu/talks/truman-g-madsen/become-like-god-highest-us/.
[71] Ibid.
[72] Ibid.
[73] Ibid.
[74] Ibid.
[75] Whitney, Orson F. as cited in *Faith Precedes the Miracle*. Deseret Book Company, Salt Lake City, 1972, p.98.
[76] Ibid.
[77] Ibid.

The education, the development, the transformation he is describing is a result of the Atonement of Jesus Christ and can only happen if we turn to Him. It is what our Savior does with our toil and tribulations. It is how He takes everything in our life and consecrates it for our gain.[79] What we gain is that education, that schooling in godliness. Trusting our Savior to transform all our experiences, even and maybe especially, the hard and horrible ones, allows our souls to expand in the face of adversity when Satan would have us shrink and shrivel. We were never meant to shoulder these things alone. If we let God support us, we receive not only the education of our sorrows but the boundless solace heaven offers. As Julie B. Beck has reminded us, "Because personal revelation is a constantly renewable source of strength, it is possible to feel bathed in help even during turbulent times."[80] We acknowledge we are to be taught by such trials, but can also be held, soothed, and come to know that God "answers privately/reaches [our] reaching."[81] "We will understand that we do not ever walk alone."[82] As President Thomas S. Monson has promised, "you will one day stand aside and look at your difficult times, and you will realize that He was always there beside you."[83]

God nurtures us with His presence.

My son, Aaron's sensory processing is unique, and I'm convinced we know very little of the actual suffering he endures daily as a result. He has found his comforts—the hums and squeals of his own voice, the way he can filter light through his moving fingers, the familiar blare of his favorite movies, and lately even some tabernacle

---

[78] Ibid.
[79] 2 Nephi 2:2
[80] Beck, Julie B. "And Upon the Handmaids in Those Days I Will Pour Out My Spirit," General Conference April 2010
[81] "Where Can I Turn For Peace?" Hymn 129, The Church of Jesus Christ of Latter-day Saints Hymnal
[82] Monson, Thomas S. "We Never Walk Alone," General Conference October 2013
[83] Ibid.

choir on his iPad. For years though, the one thing he compulsively seeks when something triggers his sensitive nervous system, is me, particularly my hair. Well-meaning professionals on his team have suggested countless substitutes, brought in hair-mimicking fidget toys, and countless dolls. But Aaron rejects them all. Sometimes his fingers graze a strand of my hair for only a moment and he is off, sufficiently regulated. Other times he seeks me out and wants to be (I admit, at times aggravatingly) close. His face, his very skull, in fact, pressed into the contours of my face, my hair shrouding us both, a makeshift holy of holies, where closeness will accept no interference.

Why do we imagine God in far-off heaven instead of with us as He has promised?[84] Do we feel at times alone, a pavilion blocking us from Him, and cry out like the Prophet, "O God, where art thou?"[85] Joseph had called on Him before, but this time there seemed to be no pillars of light appearing anytime soon. Where are you? He pleaded. When I need you now more than ever? The answer to that desperate question comes a whole section later, "Fear not for God shall be with you forever and ever."[86]

I'm right here *with* you. Not "one day this will be over and you can come and be in Heaven with me," but *right now*, Joseph, as you suffer in this place and all of its darkness, *I'm with you right now*! In that inescapable prison, Joseph heard the voice of the Lord and felt His love. His captors may have separated him from his wife, his family, and the church he led, but they could not separate him from his Master.

---

[84] Isaiah 41:10, Holy Bible, KJV.
[85] Doctrine and Covenants 121:1.
[86] Doctrine and Covenants 122:9.

The Lord told Joseph that "all these things would give him experience."[87] I've come to believe the thing we experience during our trials, *is* the love of God. In a way little else can, trials convince us of His unwavering awareness of us. It shows us who God is and what He is willing to do for us.

If we believe God uses suffering as punishment or is impatient with our weakness, we will conjure up an image of an exasperated God who may listen to our prayers, but be rolling His eyes and thinking "not again." This is not a God we trust to care for our needs. As a result, we draw near to Him with our lips, but our hearts stay far, far away.[88]

Even (and especially) when we mess up.

During my weeks spent being nurtured by God in my "garden," there were still, of course, seven (post-Covid19-quarantine, still socially distanced, missing school, missing their friends, missing their routine, needing me) children living under our, drastically reduced in size, roof. Incessant is the word that seemed best to describe their need. Without meaning to, I began to project my annoyance on God. Surely my Heavenly Parents just would love for me not to bug them for just a moment, to make my own spiritual snack without asking them to get all the ingredients out and inevitably deal with the cleanup. As mortal, imperfect parents, it can be easy to make this leap, but when we do this, we put mortal limitations upon them when it would actually be better to remember they are *so* okay with us being mortals. They made us that way! So when we mess up, it isn't just tolerated, it was anticipated and planned for.

---

[87] Doctrine and Covenants 122:7.
[88] Joseph Smith History 1:19, The Pearl of Great Price.

And man do I mess up sometimes! Just a few days ago, I threw a full-blown adult tantrum, one of my biggest yet. I had screamed and hollered in a way that would usually have drowned me in a big ol' murky pool of shame for days after. But this time, my eleven-year-old texted me, "I need a hug." Smiley face. It was the smiley face that gave him away. I found him in the kitchen, and he smirked.

"Do YOU need a hug, or do you just know that *I* do?" I asked, already starting to cry. He laughed and brought me into his man-child arms, and at that moment, he was standing in for God. Because God knew. He knew *all* the things that had swirled together to make a perfect storm that day, and He knew He could turn it into something good. He also knows the value in the opportunities we have to comfort one another, to help nurture our spiritual siblings like my kids do for one another and sometimes even me.

I love the scripture in Alma 17:10, "And it came to pass that the Lord did visit them with his Spirit, and said unto them: Be comforted. And they were comforted." We can be told, "it's okay. I love you. Be comforted." But we still have to receive it.

Gaylamarie Rosen described, "I imagine the Savior gathering us one by one and calming our fears. 'Come warm your hands by the fire of my peace and strength. I don't doubt your ability to contribute, please don't doubt My ability to strengthen you.'"[89] My son offered me mercy that day, hugging me in the kitchen. Mercy I didn't feel I deserved, but as one of my all-time favorite quotes suggests, "Surely the thing God enjoys most about being God, is the thrill of being merciful, especially to those who don't expect it and often feel they don't deserve it."[90] Elder Jeffery R. Holland continues, "however many mistakes you feel you have made or talents you think you

---

[89] Rosenberg, Gaylamarie. "Gather to Be Perfected but Not Perfect." *BYU Women's Conference*, May 1, 2020, womensconference.byu.edu/transcripts.
[90] Holland, Jeffrey R. "The Laborers in the Vineyard," General Conference April 2012

don't have, or however far from home and family and God you feel you have traveled,"[91] he testified, "you have not traveled beyond the reach of divine love."[92]

From Resisting to Resting

That initial day of discovery, laying sore in the sun, God gave me a vision of His availability and invited me to make time and space in my life for continued holy interactions. But perhaps I missed the asterisk in His lesson plan, the footnote that extrapolated further the necessary aspect of the struggle.

There were and are days, like the one I threw my epic tantrum, when I don't feel close. When, instead of focusing on God's ability to reach me, I become obsessed with the things I'm not doing, the ways I'm falling short. I feel sure that my inadequacies are what is blocking me from feeling more connected. Ironically, such inner chastisements do little to motivate me and draw me back into communion with heaven. Instead, they allowed Satan to swoop in. As author Melinda Wheelwright Brown explains, "Intellectually we understand that self-discipline is necessary for self-mastery. But we fall for the adversary's twisted implication that self-criticism is required for self-control. Research consistently shows just the opposite."[93] We act like my toddlers sometimes do when they are upset. We thrash against the very arms offering us solace. The problem is, and has been from the very beginning, that instead of going to the Lord who can embrace and encircle us, even clothe us in symbols of His redemptive, protective powers, designed to fortify us against the harshness of this lone and dreary world, we listen to

---

[91] Ibid.

[92] Ibid.

[93] Brown, Melinda Wheelwright. *Eve and Adam: Discovering the Beautiful Balance.* Narrated by Nancy Peterson, Deseret Book Company, Salt Lake City, 2020. Audiobook.

Satan who says too quickly "Hide!"[94] We grab our self-made, and rather ineffective fig leaves of shame, and end up hiding from our Creator, who is the only source of adequate help. We justify it by thinking it's what God wants us to do, despite true messengers—angelic and apostolic—declaring incessantly and emphatically, to *fear not*! Dave Butler's imagined dialogue inserted into the garden account is instructive, he adds God asking our first parents "What lies has Satan told you about me that made you think you had to hide?"[95]

> "If we let God support us, we receive not only the education of our sorrows but the boundless solace heaven offers."
>
> - Chelsea Bretzke

I remember one rather miserable 'hide from God day' when I had the thought, *what if this* (the feeling of lack I translated into unworthiness) *is just me feeling the need?* What if it's simply a signal to reach out to God, the same way my stomach grumbles when I'm hungry, or I start to yawn when I get sleepy? What if it's a divinely built-in hint: *Oh, I need some time with God?* What if, like my toddlers, I could give in and collapse exhausted into strong, loving arms that had been waiting all along?

The idea of His rest is found throughout the scriptures yet, in the past, I've tended to think of it as a thing for the next life. I'm starting to realize that the rest comes from being in his presence, and as ancient and modern scriptures reassure His disciples, we can feel that now![96] A more constant influence of his Spirit is not only what

[94] Genesis 3, Holy Bible, KJV.
[95] Butler, David. *Cultivate a Good Life: 098: Finding God in a Crazy World*. Apple Podcasts, 8 July 2020, podcasts.apple.com/us/podcast/098-finding-god-in-a-crazy-world-with-david-butler/id1438937435?i=1000483538314.
[96] St. Matthew 28:20, Holy Bible, KJV; Doctrine and Covenants 62:19.

we strive for as covenant keepers, but what our Heavenly Parents want to give us, not unlike the way we as earthly parents try to be there for our own kids. One child psychologist explained: "Children are not meant to work for love. They are meant to rest in someone's care so that they can play and grow; this is why relationships matter."[97] I believe our Heavenly Parents understand this. My wise mother-in-law once told me, as I lamented what I perceived as chaos, and she saw as just a free, safe environment to grow and develop, "They just need to know you are there for them."[98] This concept of nurturing is one I've come to adopt as my own and distills into one simple thought, they need to know you're on their side. And as we have been taught: "No one is more on our side than the Savior."[99]

God has so much to give.

God has so much light and love and mercy and hope to share. As Joseph Smith powerfully proclaimed, "Our Heavenly Father is more liberal in His views, and boundless in His mercies and blessings, than we are ready to believe or receive."[100] Once, when the prophet met with a handful of priesthood holders in the early days of the church, he asked them to share what they felt was the future of the church. After what spiraled into a bit of a session of one-upping, Joseph concluded, "I've appreciated what you've said, but you no more comprehend the destinies of this Church than a little child on its mother's lap."[101]

---

[97] MacNamara, Deborah. *Rest, Play, Grow: Making Sense of Preschoolers.* Aona Books, Vancouver, BC, 2016, p.101.
[98] Ibid.
[99] Robbins, Lynn G. "Until Seventy Times Seven," General Conference April 2018
[100] Smith, Joseph. *History, 1838–1856, Volume D-1 [1 August 1842–1 July 1843], Page 4 [Addenda].* Intellectual Reserve, Inc., 2020, www.josephsmithpapers.org/paper-summary/history-1838-1856-volume-d-1-1-august-1842-1-july-1843/285.
[101] Madsen, Truman G. "The Highest in Us." *BYU Speeches,* 4 Feb. 2020, speeches.byu.edu/talks/truman-g-madsen/become-like-god-highest-us/.

In one way, he was essentially saying "you know nothing." But babies also learn incredible amounts and have incredible instincts. My baby is at that particular age where her attachment to me is becoming very apparent. She gives me huge gummy smiles every time I look at her and cries every time I walk out of the room. She may not know very much, but she knows she belongs to me. She trusts us—her parents who gave her life—to *keep* her alive. The Parents of our Spirits know how to keep our spirits alive. They know our hearts and our heads, our psychology and complex, genetic predispositions. Every cell, every neuron, every well-worn thought path, every tired muscle, every hair on our head,[102] and every tear that falls[103] is known. So while we may not know much compared to our all-knowing Parents, we can expect...

They *will* teach us.

While Adam was offering the firstlings of the flock, an angel appeared and asked him why he was doing it. He said, "I know not, save the Lord commanded me."[104] Nephi also confessed, "I do not know the meaning of all things."[105] Sometimes we emphasize the not knowing, and forget that in BOTH instances, they are then taught by angels! They are taught of Christ. Both Adam and Eve and Nephi moved forward without knowing all things, but they did trust one thing: "I know God loveth his children."[106] The angel with Adam and Eve explained, "This thing is a similitude of the sacrifice of the Only Begotten of the Father, which is full of grace and truth."[107] The angel with Nephi showed him a vision of both Christ's earthly mission and a symbolic representation of the journey His love would take us on.

---

[102] Luke 12:7, Holy Bible, KJV.
[103] Jacob 2:35, The Book of Mormon.
[104] Moses 5:6, The Pearl of Great Price.
[105] 1 Nephi 11:17, The Book of Mormon.
[106] Ibid.
[107] Moses 5:7, The Pearl of Great Price.

When we ask God to teach us, we will be taught. We will be shown things that will change how we see everything! May we spend time in the gardens God has prepared for us, our own sacred groves, being taught by angels—true messengers—from both sides of the veil, from official pulpits and from those who covenant to minister to us with the tongue of angels, and much-needed hugs. May we, in all our learning, remember that even though we are but babes, we also know "whose [babes] we are."[108]

This is the God I want my children to know. A God who knows them. A God they can trust to not only send and raise the sun to sustain life on earth but to warm their own closed eyelids. A God who sent and raised a Son, not just to redeem a world, but to lift them from their own darkest moments. Not just a God who reigns but a God who responds. A God who we recognize from time spent in premortal life, and who longs for those moments of connection and closeness to continue even now. Yes, a God who holds us oh so close. A God who not only cares but cares for our individual souls.

I know that if we will really let God love us, lead us, nurture us; we will learn our worth, our potential, and our divinity. The love will take over. It will burn in our hearts and shine in our faces. The love will penetrate and warm all aspects of our lives, and eventually, our eternity. It will touch and sanctify every part of our soul. God has a plan. Yes, a big, all-encompassing, save all His children plan, but also, a specific plan for each of us.

Each time I have chosen to follow this plan, it has led me on an intimate journey; a quest designed to purge me and simultaneously draw forth the highest within me, to ascend and unveil the *I am* at my center, to come face to face with the God who created me, a little

---

[108] Dalton, Elaine S. "We Are Daughters of Our Heavenly Father," General Conference April 2013

god in Their glorious image[109] and who planted in me the very longing to become. This individual tutelage is designed to heal my deepest hurts, tend to my individual wellness, as well as expound upon my most profound strengths. It will take me to the edge of what He knows my heart can take, and at times, beyond. It will require profoundly personal and significant sacrifices: my version of raised blades to prayed-for sons placed on rough-hewn altars that will lead to softer altars within that offer holy promises so eternal in scope, they can sustain generations. This personal path he guides my soul on will ultimately lead me to my most personal desires and deepest dreams, not just a collective heavenly prize.

As we feel the richness of God's ever-offered nurturing love, I know we will long to do whatever it takes to feel it forever. As Sister Linda S. Reeves has taught, "...in that day of reward, we may feel to say to our merciful, loving Father, "Was that all that was required?"[110] Along with her, "I believe that if we could daily remember and recognize the depth of that love our Heavenly Father and our Savior have for us,"[111] to bask in their nurturing presence, "we would be willing to do anything to be back in Their presence again, surrounded by Their love eternally."[112]

I know that love is available to us all along our journey. It's ready to comfort us, teach us, and nourish us. My prayer is that we will recognize, accept, and flourish under the nurturing love of our Heavenly Parents. May we ever have more sense of Their care.[113]

---

[109] Genesis 1:26-7, Holy Bible, KJV.
[110] Reeves, Linda S. "Worthy of Our Promised Blessings," General Conference October 2015
[111] Ibid.
[112] Ibid.
[113] "More Holiness Give Me" Hymn 131, The Church of Jesus Christ of Latter-day Saints Hymnal

*I trust Him to give me
exactly what will help
me take my next steps
forward, to add more light
to my understanding.*

— Chelsea Bowen Bretzke —

———3———
Renee Alberts

Learning to Hear Him

"We [can] hear Him more clearly as we refine our ability to
recognize the whisperings of the Holy Ghost."[114]

President Russell M. Nelson

Throughout my life I have had experiences in feeling promptings
from the Holy Ghost—feelings of peace, comfort, stillness, and even
of warning. Yet, before ten years ago, those experiences were merely
passing moments in my life. I never took the time to notice patterns
or commonalities in how those feelings manifested within me. But,

---

[114] Nelson, Russell M. "Hear Him," General Conference April 2020

in April 2010, that changed. I learned a very hard and heartbreaking lesson that month—a lesson that became the turning point for me in wanting to *really* know what it looked like to *feel* and *hear* the whisperings of the Holy Ghost, in my life.

In March 2009, I married my husband in the Hamilton New Zealand Temple. I moved away from my home country (New Zealand) to begin life in my husband's homeland of Australia. Being in a new country with no immediate family or close friends nearby, made the move feel very foreign. I was eager to start work to distract myself from feeling homesick; I was fortunate to begin working in April 2009 as a legal secretary. However, my eager anticipated distraction left me feeling even more homesick, when I recognized almost immediately, how different the culture within the firm was than the one I was accustomed to in New Zealand.

Although the transition into work life in Australia was not what I anticipated, I felt so grateful to have crossed paths with a fellow secretary, who I will call Cristin. Cristin was warm and welcoming to me, and she became my first friend in Australia. Her heart was so big! And it matched her all-encompassing personality. Cristin was married to an Aboriginal man, and so we connected on that level because my husband is also Aboriginal. She had no children, and as we came to know each other more, Cristin opened up about the depression she faced from time to time—especially surrounding infertility. Every now and then in our conversations I would share my testimony with her of the Savior and how I know we have a loving Father in Heaven who is constantly watching over us.

There was a time that I invited Cristin to my home. It was a Saturday morning when she arrived at my front door with her big beaming smile, holding chocolate chip cookies and sachets of hot chocolate. We talked and laughed and talked some more; and then she invited me to her home that same afternoon. She drove us there, I met her husband, and then joined in on their neighborhood BBQ. That afternoon I saw an even bigger part of Cristin's heart and witnessed how much she was loved, and how she had a gift in bringing people together. We continued to be close friends.

Towards the end of April 2010, just over a year from when I started at the law firm, my team had a morning tea. On my desk sat chocolate fudge I had put aside, and as I was working a thought came into my mind — *"Go and take the chocolate fudge to Cristin and say hello to her."* At that point, I had not seen Cristin for possibly over a week. I looked up at my computer screen and thought to myself, I need to keep working; and that is what I did. A few seconds later, the exact same thought of taking the fudge to Cristin entered my mind. I again told myself I needed to keep working and rationalized that I would go and see her the next day.

The next day was a Friday, and I went up to Cristin's floor to say hello. When I arrived at her desk, the secretary that sat opposite her explained that she had taken the day off to travel to New South Wales for a wedding that day. "No worries," I thought to myself, I'll come back on Monday to see her. The weekend had come and gone, and it was another Monday morning back in the office. I arrived at work just after 8:00 am, logged into my computer, and saw an unusual email addressed to a few secretaries needing us to meet on a different level of the building. When I arrived, I saw two secretaries standing together, and one of them was crying.

"Deena, what's happening?" I asked. "You haven't heard?" she replied. "No, heard what?" I was puzzled by all the emotions. "Cristin died last Friday." If Deena said anything after that, I did not hear her. I felt like I was in a movie, where everything became a blur as I stood with such unimaginable news. My heart raced, each breath deepened, and my mind immediately went back to the Thursday before. At that moment, my heart sank as I realized—the thoughts I had to "Go and take the chocolate fudge to Cristin and say hello to her," were promptings from the Holy Ghost, but I did not recognize them. My heart was broken as tears streamed down my face.

> "As I've kept my commitment to learning how the Spirit of the Lord speaks to me, I have indeed recognized patterns in how I hear Him."
>
> - Renee Alberts

Elder Boyd K. Packer gave a talk in June 1982, and said, "The Spirit does not get our attention by shouting or shaking us with a heavy hand. Rather it whispers. It caresses so gently that if we are preoccupied we may not feel it at all."[115] The Lord knew what was going to happen. He knew I would not see Cristin again, and He tried to give me a heads up; but I was too preoccupied with what I was doing and had not *really learned* for myself (at that point) how *I* hear Him.

Elder Boyd K. Packer went on to say, "Occasionally [the Holy Ghost] will press just firmly enough for us to pay heed. But most of the time, if we do not heed the gentle feeling, the Spirit will withdraw and wait until we come seeking and listening."[116] Within that heartbreaking life lesson, I needed to forgive myself for not recognizing and heeding the promptings I received from the Holy Ghost. But, because of the experience, I made a commitment to myself that I would go forward and consciously learn how the Spirit of the Lord speaks to me. I wanted to be aware of how *I* hear Him, and to take notice of patterns and commonalities when I feel promptings from the Spirit; because "the more we diligently seek

---

[115] Packer, Boyd K. "The Candle of the Lord." *The Church of Jesus Christ of Latter-day Saints*, 25 June 1982, www.churchofjesuschrist.org/study/manual/teaching-seminary-preservice-readings-religion-370-471-and-475/the-candle-of-the-lord?lang=eng.

His voice, the easier it becomes to hear. It is not that the voice gets louder but that our ability to hear it has increased."[117]

As I have kept my commitment to consciously learn how the Spirit of the Lord speaks to me, I have indeed recognized patterns in how I hear Him. One of the patterns I became aware of is that oftentimes a "random" thought will come into my mind—while I'm driving, getting ready for the day, sitting in church, or going about daily tasks like washing the dishes. But the way I know those "random" thoughts are from the Spirit is because they often relate to something specific I've been pondering and praying about days or weeks before.

One Sunday at the beginning of this year (pre-COVID-19), I sat in the chapel with my family during fast and testimony meeting. Someone was bearing their testimony, and two of my children were fighting over who would sit on my lap. My ears could hear the words of the person speaking, but my mind and attention were with my children as I tried to manage them both, plus hold their younger brother. Then suddenly, I felt an impression come into my mind. It came as a feeling but with a rush of words that stringed together all at once— 'It's good that you're aware of your weaknesses, Renee, and that you're working on them, but you're so focused on them that you're missing your strengths. Magnify your strengths, search them out and draw from them as they will help you in the doubts you have about yourself.'

A few weeks before that moment I had been pondering over things I really desired to do. I felt like I was trying hard to strengthen my weaknesses but then felt overwhelmed and defeated by how much there was to improve. As bizarre as it may sound, drawing on my

[116] Ibid.
[117] Homer, David P. "Hearing His Voice," General Conference April 2019

strengths never crossed my mind. But I knew with a surety that the rush of words that "randomly" came to my mind were impressed upon me as a personal revelation from the Lord, giving me guidance and direction, and I was so grateful.

Are there patterns or commonalities you have recognized within your own life in how the Spirit speaks to you? "To be able to grow in personal revelation, we need to recognize how God has been speaking to us already. He has been, and is, in all the details of our lives, big and small."[118] It is so comforting to know that because we are all distinct and different in who we are, we each have a special connection with the Lord, and that connection allows us to hear Him in uniquely personal ways.

I believe the spirit of revelation is individualized to each of us. The way we feel promptings may be similar, but the experiences within those promptings are unique to each person. The Lord knows us personally and sees the desires of our hearts. Taking the time to pause and reflect on how you have heard Him in your life can create a metaphorical fountain of flowing water for you to draw from, when future revelations are impressed upon your heart and mind. Choosing to reflect on our past experiences of receiving personal revelation can help us recognize patterns in the ways we hear the voice of the Lord, and "understand how God is leading us individually to Him."[119]

Choosing faith in the Savior, Jesus Christ, gives us the space we need to hear Him, especially during times of uncertainty. Sister Joy D. Jones counseled us that, "The Lord's loving influence through the Holy Ghost helps us know His priority for our progression. Heeding personal revelation leads to personal progression. We listen and act.

---

[118] Hear Him: A Study Guide on Personal Revelation, Deseret Book Company, Salt Lake City, 2019, p.19.
[119] Ibid.

[...] Our continuing role is to receive revelation."[120] I have felt the reality of Sister Jones' words in my own life, and I believe that the Lord tutors us to hear Him in small and simple ways, to prepare our spirit for some of the most important moments of our life.

The second week of May 2020 marked one year since my fourth little one and I traveled to New Zealand to be with my younger sister. In that week, my sister had attempted to take her life; but I am eternally grateful that she is still with us today and is growing and thriving with her beautiful little girl. When I learned what had happened with my sister in May

> "Choosing faith in the Savior, Jesus Christ, allows us the space we need to hear Him, especially during times of uncertainty."
>
> - Renee Alberts

2019, I wanted to fly to New Zealand right away, but my family's circumstances at that time made flying there seem impossible. My husband and I were prayerful about what to do, and I could feel the Spirit guide me "line upon line…here a little and there a little."[121]

The first prompting I felt from the Holy Ghost was to message my best friend in New Zealand and ask her if she would visit my sister, and she did. Heeding that prompting to contact her brought peace to my heart and a remembrance of President Spencer W. Kimball's words that "God does notice us, and he watches over us. But it is usually through another person that he meets our needs."[122] As my husband and I continued seeking the Lord's guidance in prayer, and as we counseled with one another, we felt that traveling to New Zealand was what I needed to do. My husband and best friend were

---

[120] Jones, Joy D. "An Especially Noble Calling," General Conference April 2020
[121] 2 Nephi 28:30, The Book of Mormon.
[122] Kimball, Spencer W. "Small Acts of Service," December 1974 Frist Presidency Message

instrumental in my son and I going, and I witnessed once again in my life that "with God all things are possible."[123]

Unbeknownst to my sister, my son and I landed in New Zealand a few days after she had attempted to take her life. My best friend picked us up from the airport, and when we arrived at the doorstep of the respite she was in, we learned from one of the staff members on duty that my sister had tried to take her life again, an hour before we arrived. In that same moment, my sister walked out of a room that was by the front door. She looked out to where we were standing and was so surprised to see us there. It was a tender moment when we embraced each other with tear-filled eyes and as we stood there, it was re-confirmed to my spirit that I was where I needed to be.

Throughout my time in New Zealand, I was constantly praying (often in my heart), seeking guidance from my Heavenly Father to know how I could help my sister. The recurring impression I felt was to *Be still.* Every day was intense, and I did not know what I was doing. I was learning on the go, so I knew it was imperative for me to rely heavily on the Lord to help me sift through what was needful and what was not. Sister Julie B. Beck said, "The ability to qualify for, receive and act on personal revelation is the single most important skill that can be acquired in this life."[124] I am not perfect in hearing the voice of the Lord, but I know that the commitment I made to myself in April 2010—to consciously learn how the Spirit of the Lord speaks to me—had been preparing me for the weeks I was with my sister, in New Zealand.

All I wanted to do was take the pain away from my sister, but I didn't know how. Every time I'd feel at a loss of what to do, I would again feel to *Be still. Be still*—in the many thoughts that ran through

---

[123] Matthew 19:26, Holy Bible, KJV.
[124] Beck, Julie B. "And upon the Handmaids in Those Days Will I Pour Out My Spirit," General Conference April 2010

my mind each day. *Be still*—in my anticipation to have conversations with doctors and nurses. *Be still*—in quiet moments. *Be still*—when no words needed to be spoken. *Be still*—and trust that the Lord knew what was happening. *Be still*—in all the noise that was around me. "*Be still*, and know that I am God."[125] As I heeded the promptings to *Be still*, I was often given further direction from the Holy Ghost of what the next best thing was to do.

After three weeks of being with my sister, I felt the Holy Ghost prompt me that it was time to go back home to Australia. It was a subtle prompting that I felt in my heart and mind, and I wrestled with it because I did not want to leave my sister. The experiences I had during my time in New Zealand changed me in many ways—I learned about mental health, PTSD, suicide, and suicide prevention; I re-built my connection with my sister in a way that it hadn't been for years, and I grew in strengthening my relationship with the Savior—especially in hearing Him.

Saying goodbye to my sister was so hard. I knew she still had a long road ahead of her, and I wanted to stay so I could see it through *with* her. However, I knew it was important to follow the prompting I received to go home, despite what my emotions wanted to do instead. I was in tears all the way to the airport, but it was my faith in the Savior that gave me the strength to press forward. I knew He could see so much more than I could, and I needed to trust Him and His timing. When I reunited with my family, I struggled to work out how to experience joy again with them. I felt guilty if even a small part of me felt joy, and I couldn't work out how to "snap out of it." I had been with my sister every day for three weeks—always mindful of her needs first, so being present with my family and their needs was difficult for me. I was grateful we were together again, but my

---

[125] Psalms 46:10, Holy Bible, KJV. Emphasis added.

gratitude didn't *really* manifest itself because on my first full day back in Australia, my heart yearned so much to be with my sister.

I began questioning if the prompting I felt to return home was even right. I kept worrying about my sister, and my countenance was so sad. My husband and children were right in front of me. My body was with them, but *I* wasn't. Thoughts repeatedly stirred through my mind— 'Was the feeling to come back really what I felt? Or did I just convince myself that I needed to be back? Did I come back too early?' Deep down I knew the answer, but I also felt so confused. It was at that point of feeling confusion that I knew I needed to say a prayer. I went to one of our rooms, and with tears, poured out my heart to the Lord. I put aside my own feelings of emotion and desired more to be in tune with my Heavenly Father.

> *"The more we seek Him, the more we will recognize when He is speaking to us."*
>
> - Renee Alberts

When I gave myself the clearing to be still and to pray with faith, I felt clarity in my heart again that I was right where I needed to be. I felt that the personal revelation I received to fly back to Australia was also right, and that staying in a state of sadness would not serve my sister or anyone else—especially my family. I felt a clear impression upon my heart that choosing to indulge in sadness would continue to give way to doubt, frustration, not being present, and other feelings related to them which would then hinder my ability to feel and discern clearly more promptings from the Holy Ghost.

Sister Joy D. Jones said, "If we choose to focus on negative thoughts and doubt [...] instead of clinging to the Savior, it becomes difficult to feel impressions of the Holy Ghost."[126] So from that moment on, *I chose faith and to experience joy again* by recognizing and being present to the blessings the Lord had so mercifully given me—the opportunity to have had three weeks with my sister and the relationship we re-built in that time; my husband who supported me every step of the way; my best friend who was so in tune with the Spirit; close family and friends who helped take care of my little ones; my little family being kept safe when we were all apart from each other; and the increase of spiritual experiences I had, while strengthening my relationship with the Lord. "Joy comes from and because of Him."[127]

I am constantly witnessing in my life that "learning the many ways He speaks to us is a lifelong quest."[128] Have you experienced moments or seasons in your life where the heavens have felt silent? During a very trial-filled time in my life, it felt as though the heavens were closed. No matter how many faith-filled prayers I offered, and no matter how sincere my desire was to hear Him while diligently living the gospel of Jesus Christ, I could not feel a response. In that season of silence, the temptations to become frustrated, impatient, angry, annoyed, or wanting to give up on everything I knew and believed were so real, especially because the unknown fog was *so* thick. But I chose to stay in. My spirit often felt anxious as I chose to hold onto faith, because so much was unknown, but I learned that exerting faith in Jesus Christ and trusting in Him and His timing—as hard and soul stretching as it was—bore fruit that was so much sweeter than I could have ever harvested on my own.

What kept me holding onto faith in Heavenly Father and His Son, Jesus Christ, despite the heavens feeling silent? It was remembering past revelations I had received from the Holy Ghost. Choosing to

[126] Jones, Joy D. "Value Beyond Measure", General Conference April 2018
[127] Nelson, Russell M. "Joy and Spiritual Survival," General Conference October 2016
[128] Homer, David P. "Hearing His Voice," General Conference April 2019

remember that I had witnessed the Lord's hand in my life and heard Him countless times is what kept me anchored in striving to hear Him while in the fog. We need to "remember our own special spiritual experiences [because] these building blocks of faith will bring us conviction and reassurance of a caring, loving Father in Heaven, of our Lord and Savior, Jesus Christ."[129] I know that as we choose to look back and remember when we have seen the Lord's hand manifest in our lives, we will recognize spiritually defining moments that have shaped us and will sustain us through our trials, no matter how thick and unknown the fog may be.

I know for myself that Jesus Christ is the Son of God and that because of Him we have been given the constant companionship of the Holy Ghost to guide us in our lives. I know that "there may be times when you feel as though the heavens are closed,"[130] but I bear testimony that they are open, that faith precedes the miracle and that God truly does speak to His children. We are all children of God, distinct and different in so many beautiful ways. Seek to hear the voice of the Lord in your life, and be patient with yourself in the process, because it takes time. I add my witness and testimony to the words of our living prophet today, President Russell M. Nelson, that as you "continue to be obedient, expressing gratitude for every blessing the Lord gives you, and as you patiently honor the Lord's timetable, you will be given the knowledge and understanding you seek."[131]

[129] Rasband, Ronald A. "Special Experiences," General Conference May 2008
[130] Ibid.
[131] Ibid.

*Seek to hear the
voice of the Lord in your
life, and be patient with
yourself in the process,
because it takes time.*

— Renee Alberts —

—4—
Darla Trendler

Accessing Christ's Power in Your Life

In May 2019, my husband and I, and a small group of family members, accompanied our daughter to the temple for my daughter to receive her endowment. I especially remember the beautiful instruction my daughter was given by the temple matron as the three of us sat together in a small, quiet room. I felt privileged to share this experience with my firstborn. The entire time we were in the temple that day, and for days after, a phrase kept running through my mind—"endowed with power from on high."[132]

---

[132] Doctrine and Covenants 38:32

I knew this phrase was from the scriptures, so I searched and found the words in Doctrine and Covenants 38:32. This section is a revelation to Joseph Smith while he was in New York. The Lord gave Joseph instructions to go to Ohio, where the Saints would be "endowed with power from on high."[133] Later we learn that power did come to the Saints through the building of the Kirtland Temple.

Pondering on the word power continued for me after the beautiful experience watching my daughter make covenants and receive power in the temple. In October 2019, I was struck by something President Russell M. Nelson said during the women's session at general conference. The prophet reminded me that "every time you worthily serve and worship in the temple, you leave armed with God's power."[134]

My experiences of thinking about power solidified my belief that power could be found in the temple. I also studied about priesthood power, the power and authority of God, and how this power blesses both men and women. I learned even more about how I, as a woman striving to keep my covenants, can use priesthood power in my life.

But even though I was learning so much, I still wondered how I could more fully tap into the power Christ continuously offers in my life. I was seeking to share light online with other women through a podcast and Instagram account focused on helping mothers recognize God as a partner in motherhood. I felt I could use Christ's power to know how to use my podcast for good, how to be distinct and different, and how to help others come to know Him too.

There was more to know about the power from on high gained in the temple. I had more to learn about accessing the power God has for

---

[133] Ibid.
[134] Nelson, Russell M. "Spiritual Treasures," General Conference October 2019

me through the priesthood. I decided to turn to the Book of Mormon. After hearing President Nelson's invitation to prepare for the April 2020 general conference of the Church, I felt prompted to reread the Book of Mormon.

In mid-January 2020, I dove in with a fresh copy of the Book of Mormon. Since the age of nine, I had read the Book of Mormon many times all the way through and even read the whole book in a week, but I had never read the Book of Mormon from cover to cover with one single purpose in mind. This time, my reading had a specific focus—find ways to access Christ's power.

Themes started to emerge as I read. I came to find President Nelson's words to be true: "When I think of the Book of Mormon, I think of the word power."[135]

Day after day I read and wrote my thoughts and impressions. I looked for words like power, strength, might, and deliverance. I learned quickly in my reading that the people in the Book of Mormon who accessed Christ's power were showing me a pattern. I noticed over and over these people had many things in common, but I pulled out four specific things I felt particularly important for accessing Christ's power.

> They used Christ's power to accomplish great things by gaining wisdom from God instead of relying on worldly knowledge.
> They were humble. They clearly knew of their own "nothingness" and readily acknowledged they were using Christ's power and not their own.
> They had charity and used Christ's power to care for and protect others.

---

[135] Nelson, Russell M. "The Book of Mormon: What Would Your Life Be Like Without It?" General Conference October 2017

They used the power of Christ's atonement to repent and become the person God wanted them to be.

Let me show you, in detail, what I learned about each of these ways to access Christ's power.

They used God's power to accomplish great things by gaining wisdom from God instead of relying on worldly knowledge.

A few months ago, I was in a church meeting helping teenagers plan an upcoming activity for all of the youth in my stake. The youth wanted the activity to involve rotating groups of fifty-plus people. The activity had constraints on both time and space. After several minutes of brainstorming, the group hadn't come up with a solution they felt would work.

Out of nowhere, from the back of the room, I blurted out that we should have the groups stay in the same spot and have the team of teachers presenting each class rotate to the groups, thus eliminating the problem of moving large groups of people in a tight space quickly. This solution solved all of our issues and everyone quickly agreed that the idea would work great.

After the meeting, several other leaders came to me and thanked me for coming up with the "perfect solution." Because of how quickly I shared the idea and because it wasn't something I had been thinking about sharing, I knew the idea had come to me through the Spirit. I was glad we came up with a great solution, but I expressed to everyone that it wasn't actually my idea. I wasn't trying to be modest. It was true. I knew the thought I had shared was God's wisdom and not my own. I had gained wisdom and power from God at the moment I needed it, and our group was able to hold an effective activity.

In Alma 37:35, Alma explained to his son Helaman what wisdom is: "O, remember, my son, and learn wisdom in thy youth; yea, learn in thy youth to keep the commandments of God."

If gaining wisdom is learning to keep the commandments, wisdom seems to be something more than just acquiring earthly knowledge and experiences. Wisdom is learning to put aside the natural man and doing things in God's way.

Many of the examples I found in the Book of Mormon about gaining wisdom actually illustrated how *not* to do it.

For example, at one point, the Nephites suffered a huge loss to the Lamanites who had joined forces with Nephite dissenters. "And because of this their great wickedness, and their *boastings in their own strength, they were left in their own strength*; therefore, they did not prosper, but were afflicted and smitten, and driven before the Lamanites, until they had lost possession of almost all their lands."[136]

Why did the Nephites lose so badly? Their wickedness limited their wisdom. They only had access to their own power and that strength alone was not enough. (But keep reading because this story has a happy ending!)

I love to lift weights. Over years of weightlifting, I have developed a lot of strength. But sometimes my own strength gets in the way of my being able to have more power in a lift and ultimately lift more weight.

---

[136] Helaman 4:13, The Book of Mormon. Emphasis added.

My coaches frequently chide me for "muscling" a lift. My form goes out the window because I know I have enough strength in my shoulders to get the weight over my head, but my coaches correct me because "muscling" is holding me back. I could lift so much more if I would use the techniques and form my coaches have taught me. They tell me to "trust the process" but I still frequently "muscle" my way through lifts.

> "Wisdom is learning to put aside the natural man and doing things in God's way."
>
> - Darla Trendler

I find a similar pattern in my spiritual life. I frequently try to get through challenges by relying on my own strength and knowledge. I am slowly learning that I can do so much more when I rely on God's ways instead of my own ways.

The prophet Jacob taught that the Jews "despised plainness"[137] and were looking for deep things to believe in instead of simple gospel truths. Jacob revealed that the Lord gave the Jews exactly what they wanted. "...For God hath taken away his plainness from them, and delivered unto them many things which they cannot understand, *because they desired it.*"[138]

God will give you what you want. If you want to rely on yourself, you totally can, but the results may not be as extraordinary as you hoped. So much more comes when we rely on God and use His power instead of our own strength.

An early member of the church, Eliza R. Snow, explained how wisdom is the key to gaining power. She said, "Let them seek for

---

[137] Jacob 4:14, The Book of Mormon.
[138] Ibid. Emphasis added.

wisdom instead of power, and they will have all the power they have wisdom to exercise."[139] As the great prophet Jacob was wrapping up his preaching, he said one simple sentence that speaks volumes about how to access Christ's power: "O be wise; what can I say more?"[140]

Telling his people to be wise was obviously extremely important to Jacob. As I studied why wisdom was so vital to Jacob, I read Matthew 10:16 which admonishes us to be "wise as serpents, harmless as doves." This phrase reminded me of a time in my life when my boss at work received a promotion. I loved this boss. He was kind. He had nurtured me and given me many opportunities to improve. He valued my contribution to the team and listened to my opinion, even though I was in an entry-level position.

After his promotion, I got a new boss. She was crass and overly direct and had a reputation for not listening or caring about others' opinions. I didn't want to work for her, but as I prayed about how to handle the situation, this phrase came to my mind: "wise as a serpent, harmless as a dove."[141]

I knew I couldn't stoop to the ways of the world, which would mean talking behind her back and fighting against her decisions. I needed to be aware of her methods and style, but I also needed to be Christlike in how I approached her and the situation. I needed to be wise and harmless and use God's ways instead of my own to navigate the situation.

---

[139] Snow, Eliza R. Letter received by Marry Elizabeth Lightner, May 27, 1869, Church History Library, as quoted in *Daughters in My Kingdom: The History and Work of the Relief Society*, Intellectual Reserve, Inc., 2011, p.45.
[140] Jacob 6:12, The Book of Mormon.
[141] Matthew 10:16, Holy Bible, KJV.

She was only my boss for a short time, but I grew to like her and to enjoy working for her. Using God's wisdom instead of the world's helped me to navigate a difficult situation.

The prophet Moroni taught that the way to "be wise"[142] is to let go of worldly ways and "ask with a firmness unshaken,…that ye do all things in worthiness, and do it in the name of Jesus Christ, the Son of the living God…"[143]

Wisdom is also about gaining knowledge. Knowledge of God's ways helps us to have more access to His power. As Sheri Dew noted, both academic and spiritual knowledge help us "…know how to qualify for and gain access to the power of the Lord."[144]

So, if you want to have an influence on others and be distinct and different, it comes by tapping into God's power through wisdom. This is how to build influence, a form of power, in the latter days.

They were humble. They clearly knew of their own "nothingness"[145] and readily acknowledged they were using Christ's power and not their own.

If you know anything about the great missionary Ammon in the Book of Mormon, it's probably the story about how he defended a Lamanite king's flocks by cutting off the arms of the thieves who were trying to steal the sheep. The strength Ammon exhibited was extremely impressive to the Lamanites, especially the king. The power he showed quickly earned Ammon an invite to see the king and a step toward being able to share the gospel.

---

[142] Mormon 9:28, The Book of Mormon.
[143] Mormon 9:28-29, The Book of Mormon.
[144] Dew, Sheri L. *God Wants a Powerful People*. eBook. Deseret Book Company, 2010.

Ammon received praise and adoration from the Lamanites for his unprecedented strength. The king and his people recognized Ammon's strength and even said "thou art more powerful than all they."[146] But what is most impressive about Ammon is not the amazing strength he used to single-handedly defeat the king's enemies. What really makes Ammon stand out to me is what happened next. Ammon recognized and acknowledged where his might came from. He could have easily taken credit for all the incredible things he did with his strength and power, but he didn't let the accolades go to his head. He gave all the credit to the Lord saying, "I am a man...and I am called by His Holy Spirit to teach these things unto this people.... And a portion of that Spirit dwelleth in me, which giveth me knowledge and also power..."[147]

Ammon had humility. He understood that using God's power to do incredible things is a way to help others know Christ.

I can relate to the words of Moroni in the book of Ether about feeling weak in writing. As I read the Book of Mormon focusing on power, I felt so many truths about what I was learning and couldn't wait to share them. Then I sat down to write, and, like Moroni, I felt so awkward. I couldn't put on paper what I was feeling in my heart. But the Lord tells Moroni (and me) that "I give unto men weakness that they may be humble."[148]

Moroni felt comforted by the Lord's words and realized that others had done great things using God's power because they had faith. Moroni said, "...for after they had faith, and did speak in thy name, thou didst show thyself unto them in great power."[149] The Lord

---

[145] Mosiah 4:5, The Book of Mormon.
[146] Alma 18:21, The Book of Mormon.
[147] Alma 18:34-35, The Book of Mormon.
[148] Ether 12:27, The Book of Mormon.
[149] Ether 12:31, The Book of Mormon.

taught Moroni how our personal weaknesses can lead us to be humble. Moroni learned to use humility to exercise faith and tap into Christ's power.

President Nelson has counseled, "If we will humbly present ourselves before the Lord and ask Him to teach us, He will show us how to increase *our* access to *His* power."[150]

Along with Ammon's humility in giving credit to the Lord I mentioned above, Ammon also knew his own nothingness. "Yea, I know that I am nothing; as to my strength I am weak; therefore I will not boast of myself, but I will boast of my God, for in his strength I can do all things; yea, behold, many mighty miracles we have wrought in this land, for which we will praise his name forever."[151]

You may be thinking, "Does God really want me to see myself as nothing?" It seems a little counterintuitive that a loving God who views us as his children would want us to be "nothing."[152]

In a BYU devotional, M. Catherine Thomas made the distinction that nothingness isn't about our value in God's eyes. Instead, she said, "Nothingness describes...[our] powerlessness during [our] mortal probation and, especially, [our] all-encompassing need for the Lord."[153]

Nothing is not our value. Nothingness is recognizing we are in a mortal state and have an essential need for a Savior. When we recognize our nothingness, we understand that without Christ we

[150] Nelson, Russell M. "The Price of Priesthood Power," General Conference April 2016
[151] Alma 26:12, The Book of Mormon.
[152] 1 Corinthians 13:1-3; Romans 7:8, Holy Bible, KJV.
[153] Thomas, M. Catherine. "The Doer of Our Deeds and the Speaker of Our Words." *BYU Speeches*, 7 Dec. 1993, speeches.byu.edu/talks/m-catherine-thomas/doer-deeds-speaker-words/.

have no power to overcome death and sin. We must access Christ's power to return to, and become like Father in Heaven.

In an address to his people, King Benjamin taught about the importance of knowing your own "nothingness."[154] He said when you know you can't do anything on your own and that Christ is the one providing "...his matchless power, and his wisdom, and his patience, and his long-suffering...and also, the atonement, this is how you will be saved."[155] Knowing you have

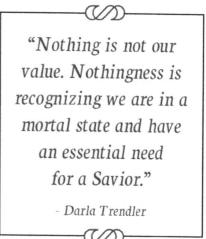

"Nothing is not our value. Nothingness is recognizing we are in a mortal state and have an essential need for a Savior."

- Darla Trendler

no power on your own is, paradoxically, how you can access Christ's power. Christ is the only way.

They had charity and used Christ's power to care for and protect others.

In the Book of Mormon, Captain Moroni is described as "a strong and a mighty man."[156] He could be an example of many of the traits of people who access Christ's power in the Book of Mormon, but one thing he really excelled in was caring for others above himself. Captain Moroni clearly was constantly working on possessing the Christlike attribute of charity, the pure love of Christ.

Captain Moroni gave all of his energy and found "joy in the liberty and the freedom of his country, and his brethren from the bondage of

---

[154] Mosiah 4:5, The Book of Mormon.
[155] Mosiah 4:6, The Book of Mormon.
[156] Alma 48:11, The Book of Mormon.

slavery."[157] He wasn't a great military leader because he enjoyed bloodshed. Moroni was remarkable because of his strong desire to serve others by protecting them physically and spiritually. Captain Moroni "did not delight in murder or bloodshed, but he delighted in the saving of his people from destruction."[158]

In this section of the Book of Mormon, we also see someone who was the exact opposite of Captain Moroni. While Moroni was seeking to protect physically and fortify spiritually, Amalickiah, a Nephite traitor, didn't care for his people and used "fraud and deceit"[159] to gain power. While Captain Moroni was motivated by his love of Christ, Amalickiah was propelled forward by aligning himself with Satan.

Amalickiah's quest to secure power from Satan brought his people misery and led to his own death, with a javelin in his heart. On the other hand, Captain Moroni's story teaches us that having charity and using Christ's power to help defend others eliminates Satan's power.

As Mormon was abridging the plates the Book of Mormon was written on, he summed up Captain Moroni's influence in this way. "Yea, verily, verily I say unto you, if all men had been, and were, and ever would be, like unto Moroni, behold, the very powers of hell would have been shaken forever; yea, the devil would never have power over the hearts of the children of men."[160]

During Ammon's mission to the Lamanites, Abish, a Lamanite woman and servant of the Lamanite King Lamoni, saw an opportunity to help others by showing them God's power. Abish had

---

[157] Ibid.
[158] Alma 55:19, The Book of Mormon.
[159] Alma 48:7, The Book of Mormon.
[160] Alma 48:17, The Book of Mormon.

already been secretly converted to the gospel. She knew why the king and the king's wife had fallen to the ground after hearing Ammon preach and pray. They had been overcome by the Spirit and converted to Christ. Abish saw an opportunity to help the rest of the people see God's power.

She started to gather the people together so they could see what was happening. She hoped that by seeing, they too would be converted, but the people only became contentious. Abish used Christ's power to touch the queen and raise her up. The queen touched the king and he rose and taught the people what Ammon had taught him, and when they heard his testimony, many were converted.

To me, the story of Abish is an example that shows it's not just prophets, missionaries, and people who are well known who can access and use Christ's power to help others. Abish was a servant, but she had access to use Christ's power as well. You and I have that same access! Charity is a gift all have the ability to develop, no matter who you are, where you live, or what your calling is. As Nephi taught, "...he inviteth them all to come unto him and partake of his goodness; and he denieth none that come unto him...and all are alike unto God..."[161]

The Prophet Joseph Smith noted that in addition to blessing his or her own family, a person who has charity "...ranges through the whole world, anxious to bless the whole human race."[162]

They used the power of Christ's atonement to repent and become who God wanted them to be.

---

[161] 2 Nephi 26:33, The Book of Mormon.
[162] Smith, Joseph. History of the Church of Jesus Christ of Latter-day Saints, 4:227. Edited by B.H. Roberts, 7 vols. 2nd ed. Rev. Intellectual Reserve, Inc., Salt Lake City, 1932-51.

Last year, I woke one morning after having a very vivid dream. A scene from my life as a young adult 23 years earlier had been replayed in the dream. The real-life experience I dreamed about had taught me that if I gave up something I wanted and thought was right for me, God had so much more in store for me.

Since dreams usually involve things that haven't actually happened, I wondered why I had dreamed of an actual event in my life. A very clear thought came to my mind: "What do I need to give up so I can have more?"

Through prayer and pondering, I felt this was a message God wanted me to understand. There was something in my life He wanted me to let go of because He had more He wanted to give me. I soon had a prompting to check the label of a drink I regularly consumed. The ingredients didn't feel right to me, so even though I literally stored cases of this drink in my closet, I gave it up.

President Nelson shared this thought when he talked about getting away from worldly things. He said, "You will need to say no to some things, even though they may seem harmless."[163] Giving up a drink was a start, but what I realized as I pondered, studied, and sought for personal revelation was there was more the Lord wanted me to know.

I began to understand the thing He wanted me to give up was sin. Sin was what was keeping me from the Savior's power and from being who God wanted me to be. In the past, I had viewed sin as something for people who did really bad things, but the Spirit taught me I needed to change my view of sin.

---

[163] Nelson, Russell M. "Spiritual Treasures," General Conference October 2019

I clearly fell into the camp of church members who Elder David A. Bednar described when he said we know that Christ atoned for "sinners" but we may not realize that He also provided His atonement "for saints—for good men and women who are obedient, worthy, and ... striving to become better."[164] I started to understand that repentance wasn't something negative. As the new Young Women theme states, I could "cherish the gift of repentance and seek to improve each day."[165]

Repentance was cherished and brought great power to a group of Lamanites who became known as the people of Ammon, or the Anti-Nephi-Lehis. "...the work of the Lord did commence among the Lamanites...the Lord did begin to pour out His Spirit upon them..."[166]

Prior to receiving and accepting the gospel through Ammon and his brethren, this group of people had committed many sins including a great deal of bloodshed. But once they were converted, they repented and sought to be who God wanted them to be. They found power in the atonement of Jesus Christ and in making a covenant with God. They were even willing to lose their lives to keep, rather than break, the covenants they had made.

Let's talk about Ammon again. I know I keep coming back to him, but to me, Ammon is one of the greatest examples in the Book of Mormon of someone who knew how to access Christ's power.

After years of missionary work, Ammon was so happy to be reunited with his brothers and fellow missionaries. He shared with them how

---

[164] Bednar, David A. "In the Strength of the Lord." *BYU Speeches*, 23 Oct. 2001, speeches.byu.edu/talks/david-a-bednar/strength-lord/.

[165] "Young Women Theme." *The Church of Jesus Christ of Latter-day Saints*, Nov. 2019, www.churchofjesuschrist.org/study/new-era/2019/11/young-women-theme?lang=eng.

[166] Alma 19:36, The Book of Mormon.

repentance gives us power. He said someone who is not trying to repent is not going to know the power of God. But someone who "repenteth and exerciseth faith, and bringeth forth good works, and prayeth continually without ceasing—unto such it is given to know the mysteries of God."[167] I think when Ammon mentions that someone who repents can know the mysteries of God, he is saying that person can use God's power. Ammon continues talking to his brothers and tells them not only will repentance and the other things he listed lead to knowing how God works, but it will also help them teach others to repent as well.

> "God sent all of us to experience a mortal life and while we can't return to Him on our own, He provided a way for us to access His power."
>
> - Darla Trendler

Earlier, I talked about the Nephites who were beaten in a battle with the Lamanites because they relied on their own strength and didn't use Christ's power. If you keep reading, you will find just a few verses later that all was not lost for these Nephites. The Lord never gives up on us and even if we have not sought to access His power in the past, there is still hope.

After their defeat, we learn that this group of Nephites was taught by Moronihah, as well as Helaman's sons, Nephi and Lehi. The Nephites, who had previously only relied on themselves, learned how to repent. "...[T]hey did repent, and inasmuch as they did repent they did begin to prosper."[168] As President Nelson has said, "Covenant-keeping men and women seek for ways to keep

---

[167] Alma 26:22, The Book of Mormon.
[168] Helaman 4:15, The Book of Mormon.

themselves unspotted from the world so there will be nothing blocking their access to the Savior's power."[169]

Jesus Christ Teaches Us How to Gain His Power

Jesus Christ is the central figure of the Book of Mormon. The people I learned from in the Book of Mormon knew and followed Him.

I am grateful for these people of the Book of Mormon who have taught me so beautifully how to access the power of Jesus Christ more fully in my life through wisdom, humility, nothingness, charity, and repentance.

Jesus Christ taught us the power of his wisdom when he declared, "...my wisdom is greater than the cunning of the devil."[170] When we turn to the Savior, we have more power than Satan, and we don't have to succumb to his temptations. When we reject Christ, we give the adversary power to control us.

Through Christ's words to Moroni, he showed us that humility gives us strength: "And because thou hast seen thy weakness thou shalt be made strong..."[171] Our weaknesses have a purpose. They help us to turn to Him and use His power to become more than we are on our own. Weaknesses make us stronger.

The Savior told the Nephites, "Yea, blessed are the poor in spirit who come unto me, for theirs is the kingdom of God."[172] King

---

[169] Nelson, Russell M. "Drawing the Power of Jesus Christ into Our Lives," General Conference April 2017

[170] 3 Nephi 21:10, The Book of Mormon.

[171] Ether 12:37, The Book of Mormon.

[172] 3 Nephi 12:3, The Book of Mormon.

Benjamin described what "poor in spirit"[173] means when he said his people, after hearing about the meaning of Christ's atonement, "viewed themselves in their own carnal state."[174] Christ is telling us power doesn't come from ourselves, and we really are nothing without Him. This knowledge leads to obtaining the kingdom of heaven and Christ's power.

Nothingness, a recognition of reliance on the Savior, is also related to charity. As Moroni wrote in his final words in the Book of Mormon, "...if ye have not charity, ye are nothing, for charity never faileth. Wherefore, cleave unto charity, which is the greatest of all, for all things must fail—But charity is the pure love of Christ, and it endureth forever...".[175] Jesus is the ultimate example of charity. As Elder Jeffrey R. Holland put it, *True* charity has been known only once. It is shown perfectly and purely in Christ's unfailing, ultimate, and atoning love for us."[176] Christ invites us to follow Him and receive the power of His love that never ends.

Christ's power makes it possible for each of us to repent. The invitation the Savior gave to the Nephites is also for us: "Therefore, whoso repenteth and cometh unto me as a little child, him will I receive, for of such is the kingdom of God. Behold, for such I have laid down my life and have taken it up again; therefore repent and come unto me ye ends of the earth, and be saved."[177]

The Savior "hath power given unto him from the Father to redeem them from their sins because of repentance...which bringeth unto the power of the Redeemer, unto the salvation of our souls."[178] Through

---

[173] Ibid.
[174] Mosiah 4:2, The Book of Mormon.
[175] Moroni 7:46-47, The Book of Mormon.
[176] Holland, Jeffrey R. *Christ and the New Covenant*, Deseret Book Company, Salt Lake City, 1997, p.336.
[177] 3 Nephi 9:22, The Book of Mormon.
[178] Helaman 5:11, The Book of Mormon.

His power we have the ability to repent and ultimately return to Father.

After my focused study of power in the Book of Mormon, I have faith and hope that I will no longer "...put down the power and miracles of God..."[179] But I will remember I am not alone. God sent all of us to experience a mortal life and while we can't return to Him on our own, He provided a way for us to access His power. You and I can be "endowed with power from on high."[180] We can attend the temple and understand priesthood power more fully. We can remember the words of our prophet, President Nelson: "The gospel of Jesus Christ is filled with His power, which is available to every earnestly seeking daughter or son of God."[181]

---

[179] 2 Nephi 26:20, The Book of Mormon.
[180] Doctrine and Covenants 38:32
[181] Nelson, Russell M. "Drawing the Power of Jesus Christ into Our Lives," General Conference April 2017

So much more comes
when we rely on
God and use His power
instead of our own strength.

— Darla Trendler —

—5—
Audra Elkington

Becoming a Spokeswoman for the Lord

As I stood there surrounded by curtains and cables and people trying to get their job done, all I could think was "Help me, I'm so nervous." The next thing I knew I was walking onto the stage with a microphone attached to my ear. I was afraid to let out my breath because I didn't want to be the speaker who was a noisy breather! The lights were so bright I could not see beyond the front row of the audience, but I knew that beyond the glare were more than 1,500 people. As I opened my mouth to begin speaking, a gentle voice in my head reminded me that this was for them. Someone hidden in those bright lights needed the message I was about to share. They needed to hear that being centered in Christ could be messy and imperfect.

The ten minutes I spent on stage at *Time Out for Women-Raleigh* taught me a few lessons, the first one being that when I am on the Lord's errand, I will be given the courage needed to fulfill the task. I also learned that I need to help the one (but usually there is more than one) who will be impacted when I share my story. And third, all the trials and experiences I have had are all the ways the Lord has taught me to come closer to Him. By sharing that with others, I am helping them find Him too.

Russell M. Nelson, President of the Church of Jesus Christ of Latter-day Saints, has said, "True disciples of Jesus Christ are willing to stand up, speak up and be different from the people of the world."[182] At times, sharing testimony and the truths I hold close to my heart can feel scary, like I am setting myself up to be ridiculed. But the Lord does not bless us with truth and knowledge so we can confine it to the pages of our own journals. He asks each of us to be a spokesperson for Him—to help others find Him.

I know the story of Esther in the Old Testament is a favorite among Christian women. Quite honestly, I could not have told you Esther's story until this year. Now, however, I understand why it's a favorite because it has become my favorite too.

It was just this year that I realized that Esther is me. She is probably you too. In fact, each year at the start of Purim—the celebration of their freedom—the Jews read the Book of Esther. It calls them to the remembrance of all that they, as a people, have been through. Heavenly Father does this for each of us in countless ways. He wants us to be called to the remembrance of the great things He has brought us through. And maybe this is why He woke me from my

---

[182] Nelson, Russell M. "Drawing the Power of Jesus Christ into Our Lives," General Conference April 2017

hazy sleep, early one December morning, to invite me to read the Book of Esther.

I was born into and raised a member of the Church of Jesus Christ of Latter-day Saints. I checked all the boxes of a Latter-day Saint young woman, well into my twenties. Looking at my outward appearance, no one could have guessed the internal struggle I was having. Satan was working hard to convince me that I was nothing, that I was all alone in this world, that I was a horrible mother, that my husband didn't want to be married to me, that I was not the daughter or sister my family needed, that my body was not fit enough, that I wasn't a good enough photographer, that I was wasting my college degree. He won. I believed every single lie he told me. We meet Esther when she is in a similar situation. She was an orphan, "she had neither father nor mother."[183] And on top of that, she was a Jew. She belonged to a people that were mocked and hated.

By the time I had my second child at the age of 30, I had been through multiple miscarriages and suffered from postpartum depression and anxiety. I had also been through several moves around the United States, had experienced unemployment, and was struggling to keep my marriage afloat with a husband who never seemed to be home. I was in the beginning stages of disordered eating behaviors, in debt, and really had no clue what I believed in. I hoped that God was real but was completely uncertain of how He fit into my life. I sat in this space for close to a decade.

And then my personal Mordecai walked in. Mordecai took in his cousin's daughter, Esther. He gave her a place with his family. He recognized "the maid was fair and beautiful."[184] He saw her inherent value. As I read through Esther's story, Mordecai became a representation of anyone in my life (both on Earth and on the other side of the veil) who has helped me to see my worth as a child of

---

[183] Esther 2:7, Holy Bible, KJV
[184] Ibid.

God. A loving Heavenly Father sent people to gently guide me back to Him. I did not go looking for the Savior, just as Esther did not go looking for a spot in the King's court. And yet, somehow, I found myself sitting in the space God needed me to be in. He compelled my family to move to a new city, a place where we could have a fresh start. He knew that, in such a situation, I would be more willing to hear what the Spirit was telling me.

The road to stepping into our God-given purpose is not easy. Even when we have had our "A-ha" moment, the moment where we discover that we *are* doing what we agreed to in our premortal life, there is plenty of room to doubt ourselves. Like Esther, we have to go through our own purification process. The process can be long and not always pleasant. In Esther 2:12 we read:

> *Now when every maid's turn was come to go in to king Ahasuerus, after that she had been twelve months, according to the manner of the women, (for so were the days of their purifications accomplished, to wit, six months with oil of myrrh, and six months with sweet odors, and with other things for the purifying of the women;)*

Esther had to wait patiently for twelve months for her purification to be completed. She had to go through six months of healing with myrrh oil—the oil used to anoint Kings. And then six more months being treated with sweet odors and other things.

What I learn from Esther's purification process has helped me to better understand what it means to wait on the Lord. Sometimes our purifying experiences will be for our own healing, sometimes we will experience sweet things, like tender mercies. However, it's the other things that draw my attention. Purifying is not always healing. It's not always a tender mercy from God in the moment.

Sometimes purifying looks like fighting my way through resentment over the fact that no matter how hard I try to maintain a peace-filled home, contention finds its way into scripture study with my children.

It looks like helping my middle child claw her way through a severe anxiety disorder. It is me trying my hardest to not be bitter about whatever difficult and unresolvable circumstance I find myself in. And it is me, even after all of my sacred experiences with the Savior, still finding myself feeling like I am just not good enough. Purification takes time. Sometimes we continue to fight the same battle for days, months, or years on end with no resolution in sight.

But here is a valuable lesson I learned from Esther. Even after she made it to the house of the maidens, even after she went through her purification, the fact still remained that she was a Jew. At the time, some in the King's court believed that the Jewish laws were not in accordance with the laws of the land. This led some to think that the Jews were a hindrance or threat to the King and his people. And yet, "the king loved Esther above all the women, and she obtained grace and favor in his sight more than all the virgins; so that he set the royal crown upon her head."[185] In spite of the fact that she could not remove her main burden, her Jewish heritage, Esther was beloved by the king. And so it is with each of us. The Lord knows our weaknesses. He also knows that we are still undergoing our own purification process. He accepts us right where we are. He loves us right where we are. He knows where He wants to take us.

Heavenly Father is well aware of the fact that one of my main challenges in life right now is not something that I can resolve. My only option is to choose love, every...single...day. But sometimes, choosing love is hard. Sometimes, choosing love means our best intentions are rejected by those we are closest to.

Continuing with Esther's story, while Esther was enjoying the perks of being a new queen, her people were in mourning. King Ahasuerus had been urged by his kingsman, Haman, to destroy all the Jews in the land. Haman's reasoning was that the Jews were a hindrance and burden to the kingdom. At this point, Esther still had not revealed

---

[185] Esther 2:17, Holy Bible, KJV

her heritage and the decree for the Jews to be killed was still valid. At one point, Esther's maids saw Mordecai in his sackcloth—the token of mourning and a sign of submission. Esther, loving Mordecai for all he'd done for her, sent him some new clothes to try to lift his spirits. But "he received it not."[186] Esther could have chosen to be offended that her gift was not received in the way she had hoped. She could have decided right then and there to give up on trying to help Mordecai. Instead, Esther chose "to know what it was, and why it was."[187] She asked questions because she wanted to understand.

I can choose to be bitter, sad, or resentful about my current circumstances. They are hard. I am sure many, if not all of you, feel the same way about a challenge or two in your own life. Anyone you talk to would give you permission to wallow in negative emotion. But, that is not what the Lord wants us to choose. That is not what Esther chose to do. She chose to love. She chose to try to understand someone else. And it was through asking questions that Esther came to know her own purpose. While showing love and trying to help Mordecai, he revealed Esther's true identity by asking her this question, "and who knoweth whether thou art come to the kingdom for such a time as this?"[188]

With that one question Esther's understanding (of who she was and what her purpose was) shifted. That is how the Savior helps each of us. When we put aside our negative emotions and truly seek to love as He does, we open ourselves up to being shown how He sees us. Carri P. Jenkins has said: "Esther's mettle—or, some would say, her self-confidence—was far more than a strong personality: it was the direct result of putting her trust, faith, and reliance in the Lord."[189]

---

[186] Esther 4:4, Holy Bible, KJV

[187] Esther 4:5, Holy Bible, KJV

[188] Esther 4:14, Holy Bible, KJV

[189] Jenkins, Carri P. "A Solemn Obligation." *BYU Speeches*, 8 Nov. 2005, speeches.byu.edu/talks/carri-p-jenkins/solemn-obligation/.

Once we become aware of who we truly are and what our purpose is we have to take the next step. We have to get moving! Knowing who we are meant to be does nothing for us unless we take action. Jenkins went on to say: "Our Father in Heaven will guide you, help you, and support you. He does not want you to put your light under a bushel; instead, He wants you to put it on a candlestick where it cannot be hid."[190]

The first thing Esther did was acknowledge that God had, in fact, put her in a position to be the Queen because He had a work for her to do. After acknowledging this deliberate placement, she took action herself and encouraged others to act. She told Mordecai to "Go and gather together all the Jews that are present...and fast ye for me...I also and my maidens will fast likewise."[191] She knew that sitting around thinking about this new revelation could not save her or her people.

"He wants us to be called to the remembrance of the great things He has brought us through."

- Audra Elkington

When God reminded me that He was there with me all the time, even in my personal wilderness, He knew that I would need something to help me remember He was there. In a way that was *not* subtle He told me to trust Him and go back to church. And so I did, dragging my three unaware children with me. God knew that I would need church, and the people I would find there, to keep me encouraged to continue on the path He had set for me. He knew I would need the reminder of partaking of the Sacrament each Sunday. He also knew that He would need to give me courage and conviction to share my

---

[190] Ibid.
[191] Esther 4:16, Holy Bible, KJV

experiences and what I was learning so that I could help others to see His hand in their own lives. But, the first action I needed to take was to simply go to church. He does not expect us to reach His end goal in one step. He is a God who teaches His children line upon line so we do not become overwhelmed.

Like Esther, performing one small action gave me the courage and strength I needed to perform the next action. Esther knew that anyone who entered the king's chambers without being called for would perish. And yet she proclaimed, "...so will I go in unto the king, which is not according to the law: and if I perish, I perish."[192] How often do you feel called to do something but get scared because you are caught up thinking about all the repercussions? I used to be so terrified of negative consequences from my choices. I am a people pleaser; I hate to disappoint people. But if I am ever going to move forward and do the work God has for me, I have to let go of my need to please everyone. Pleasing everyone will never be possible.

Recently, at the start of a new year, I decided that if something brought light to my life I was going to say "yes" no matter what the ramifications would be. Did I disappoint people? I am sure I did. But what I discovered was that when I was doing something that felt right to me, I truly quit caring about any negative comments. Also, I was able to quickly brush myself off when I was told "no." In fact, the roadblocks of being told "no," or getting pushback actually fueled me to continue saying "yes." I became more courageous as I realized that negativity was actually Satan trying to prevent me from doing something good. This knowledge helps me understand how Esther was able to truthfully say she didn't care if she perished in the process of trying to save her people. Courage comes when we are on the right path.

Courage, however, does not equal mission accomplished. What courage does do is give us that little push we need to take the next

---

[192] Ibid.

step. It gives us the confirmation we need to keep choosing to do what the Lord is asking of us. After I had been going back to church each week for a couple of months, the next action showed up in the form of a calling to serve in the Young Women organization. I knew that this was almost an easy "yes" from the Lord. He had just asked me to do something hard, so I felt like this was my reward for doing that hard thing. I love teenagers. Most of my friends loved the baby and toddler years, but I always knew that parenting teens is when I would truly feel in my element. The Lord knew this and so He was handing me an opportunity to say "yes" to something that would not only move me closer to where He needed me to be, but it would allow me to be more in my comfort zone while He worked on me for a bit longer.

The next thing Esther did, after declaring her hard thing, was to put on her royal apparel before she entered the king's court. Putting on our clothes is habitual. Most people don't even realize that they put on their clothing the same way every single time. Right leg then left. Arms in sleeves, then shirt over their head. Without thinking, we get dressed in the way we have grown most comfortable with. Not only were Esther's dressing habits comforting, but she also had the added reminder that she was made queen—her royal robes gave her the reminder that even though she was once an orphan, she had been put in a situation where she had power. How much courage this must have given her to proceed to the next hard thing!

As I look back on all that has taken place in my life the past two and a half years, I find myself looking for the things that have given me the courage to continue taking the next step on the path the Lord has set before me. My list is topped by the fact that two of my three children made the decision to be baptized within eighteen months of attending church again. I have built friendships with people who continually see the good in me and encourage me to choose the next right step. Having the responsibility for teaching the youth motivates me to continue my personal daily studies. I have found peace in my marriage that was not there before. When we actively seek to see the comfort the Lord gives, He will show himself in the things we think seem too simple. The things that we do routinely without giving them much thought.

But, oh how we need simple things to build our faith and courage, because there are always bigger things waiting in the wings. Esther knew that the next thing she had to do was enter the king's court and wait for him to beckon her or be put to death. What a daunting task! As I studied this part of Esther's story, I became curious to understand the significance of the king and his scepter. What I discovered was a lesson that will stick with me and which helped open my eyes to better understand an eternal truth. The scepter was a rod or staff that a king held to indicate that he was the authority figure—the shepherd of his people. Symbolically speaking, we can liken the king and his scepter to the Savior and the power of His Atonement. The Savior offers His atoning power to each of us. It is up to us to simply reach out and touch it. Without the courage Esther had already built up, would she have had the faith to accept the king's offering? I do not think without all the comforting experiences I have had the past couple of years, I would have the courage to pursue the things I feel the Lord is compelling me to do. Sure, He is asking me to do some pretty amazing things. But I doubt I would have found them so amazing two years ago when my faith and my courage were so weak. Nor would I have recognized them as opportunities from the Lord to have me do the work He wants me to do.

The Lord knows this. He knows that He cannot ask us to do the big things before we're ready. This is where we see His mercy in abundance—teaching us one step at a time is one of the greatest blessings He gives us. "Confronting the king at the risk of her life did not make Esther courageous; rather, it revealed the courage that was within her—the courage, the compassion, the devotion to her

94

people."[193] Once Esther realized her divine potential, once she received acceptance from the king, she did not hesitate to take the next step. From that moment on, she proceeded with courage and a strong conviction that she had a purpose to fulfill.

I have had those moments. Those moments where I feel the Lord's acceptance and that acceptance has given me all the strength I need. Strength and courage to continue acting on the things He requires of me; the things that He knows only I can do. In Esther 7:3 we read, "If I have found favour in thy sight, O king, *and*, if it please the king, let my life be given me at my petition, and my people at my request."[194] I love the "AND." Esther knew that her request was a righteous desire, but she also knew that it needed to be pleasing to the king.

I think of all the times that my requests of the Lord were good, but they weren't what the Lord had in mind for me. During my years of dealing with infertility and multiple miscarriages, I begged and pleaded for a baby. I knew it was a righteous desire. The Lord has commanded us to have children and raise them to be disciples of Christ. Yet, the Lord also knew what was coming my way. He knew that when my husband was laid off from his job and we had to suddenly move away from friends and a life we loved, that was the time I would need my sweet middle child. He knew that giving birth to that long-awaited daughter was exactly what my heart would need to make it through those months of feeling lonely and sad about what I had left behind. He also knew the experiences I would need that would force me to learn how to lean on Him instead of someone else.

My personalized life circumstances, hand-crafted by a loving Heavenly Father, have helped me choose the Savior every single day because I want to choose Him, not because it is expected of me.

---

[193] Smith, Barbara B. " '. . . For Such a Time as This.' " *BYU Speeches*, 16 Feb. 1982, speeches.byu.edu/talks/barbara-b-smith/time/.
[194] Esther 7:3, Holy Bible, KJV. Emphasis added.

While our desires might be good, we must remember the "AND" that pleases Him. We often make plans for our lives that would appear to set us on a path the Lord would smile upon, "but other essential growth and a more profound joy can often come from adjusting our hopes to an altered and perhaps eternal plan."[195]

Esther realized that her decision to boldly go to the king and make her request would be life altering. But she also realized that the impact of the king's decision would last so much longer than that one scary moment. And so she acted. She knew that she had to be bold in order for the king to see the truth, she also knew that she had to use her influence for good. She could not let her position be wasted. "...And Mordecai came before the king; for Esther had told what he was unto her...And Esther set Mordecai over the house of Haman."[196] Esther used her position of power to shine a light on Mordecai, the person who had helped her to become who she was meant to be.

This is what is expected of each of us. Once we understand who we truly are, once we realize our divine nature, God expects us to speak up and to help bring others to Him so that they, too, can discover their own divine nature. Speaking of Esther, Barbara B. Smith said: "Her selfless allegiance...inspires our dedication and loyalty today. In this way her life was not for one time only but a legacy to succeeding generations and peoples. Great lives have enduring impact."[197]

We all have "great lives." Sometimes we just need to be reminded, to have our greatness pointed out to us by other people. This is why who we surround ourselves with matters so much. In Esther's case, she could have chosen to buddy up with Haman. He was the king's right-hand man and it would have been in Esther's favor to have

[195] Smith, Barbara B. " '. . . For Such a Time as This.' " *BYU Speeches*, 16 Feb. 1982, speeches.byu.edu/talks/barbara-b-smith/time/.
[196] Esther 8:2, Holy Bible, KJV.
[197] Smith, Barbara B. " '. . . For Such a Time as This.' " *BYU Speeches*, 16 Feb. 1982, speeches.byu.edu/talks/barbara-b-smith/time/.

Haman on her side. Instead, Esther chose to remain faithful to and kept company with Mordecai. He was the person who took her in when she was at her lowest and who encouraged her and was always honest with her, even when it meant she would have to do something incredibly difficult. Those with the right connections or with the power to make decisions are not always the right people for us. Stay in tune with how you truly feel when you are around people. The Spirit will guide you to the individuals who will help you become who you are meant to be.

There have been so many women who have had a lasting impact on me because they lived boldly. They were unafraid to share their own "great lives." As we watch other women confidently serve and go forth, we can learn by their example and draw on their strength to help us in our own lives. Barbara B. Smith said: "Esther's great contribution to her people was made not as a climactic achievement of a long-pursued goal, but as an indication of her readiness to respond to a current crisis."[198]

I am positive that each of us makes decisions each day that can be considered great contributions. For example:

As a mother, waking up countless times each night to assure a child that they are being watched over.

As a wife, moving all over the country so your husband can pursue his career ambitions or working while he pursues a degree.

As a friend, dropping your to-do list to go sit with a friend who needs a listening ear.

As a disciple of Christ, praying daily to know how you can bring someone to know Him.

As a teacher, facilitating faith-building and safe conversations.

As a daughter of God, choosing to share your story because you know your vulnerability will encourage others.

---

[198] Ibid.

I don't think we can be reminded enough of just how important those seemingly small, daily decisions are. Even Esther, who knew she had already gained the favor of the king, had to be reminded that his grace was still being extended to her. After she had already petitioned him and made her request for her people to be saved, she still continued to experience the king holding out his scepter. "Then the king held out the golden sceptre toward Esther. So, Esther arose, and stood before the king."[199]

> "The Spirit is constantly reminding me that He did not give me an increase of knowledge and courage just to keep it to myself."
>
> - Audra Elkington

The Lord continually reaches out to each of us in a similar manner. He knows that confidence and certainty don't stick around, even after we have experienced the great things in our lives. We are continually needing His grace, His acceptance, His encouragement to keep building our courage. His hand is always extended to us but, like Esther, it is up to us to reach out and grab it. It is in the act of reaching for His outstretched arms that we "...develop the intellectual integrity and spiritual strength which will be a reservoir sufficient to meet each challenge with knowledge and testimony..."[200] Smith then encourages us to seek and hold tight to precious truths. These truths will give us the courage and confidence to overcome obstacles.

We become more courageous as we draw upon our own personal reservoirs. These experiences help us to stand up for truth and be more bold. Once we have been strengthened, we are better able to extend a token of mercy to those around us who are in need of help,

---

[199] Esther 8:4, Holy Bible, KJV.
[200] Smith, Barbara B. " '. . . For Such a Time as This.' " *BYU Speeches*, 16 Feb. 1982, speeches.byu.edu/talks/barbara-b-smith/time/.

to those who don't yet have enough courage to stand on their own, or maybe those who are not in a position to be heard.

Mordecai did this for Esther by giving her a safe place to grow up and then encouraging her to set her sights on becoming queen. It was because of Esther's courage that an entire group of people were saved from slaughter and set free. Not only were they set free, but they were able to use Esther's show of courage to find the strength within themselves to go out and turn away their enemies.

Each of us is asked to do the same. In a speech given at Brigham Young University in 2005, Carri P. Jenkins proclaimed, "...each one of us has the ability and the obligation to testify and defend the work of the Lord. I beg you not to lean away or drop your voice in these situations."[201] Jenkins goes on to encourage us to take note of the people around us and use our own strengths to meet their needs.

As I have regained my footing in the gospel of Jesus Christ, I have come to know Him in a way I never have before. I am finally beginning to understand His grace, mercy, unfailing love, and how He ministers to each individual. I have gained confidence unlike anything I have ever felt, which has allowed me to continue to put my trust in Him, especially when I am unsure of the next step. I have also felt a keen sense of responsibility placed upon my shoulders. The Spirit is constantly reminding me that He did not give me an increase of knowledge and courage just to keep it to myself. It is meant to be shared with others, to be an example of how He works in our lives.

The more women who are willing to speak up and teach about how the Lord works in their lives from day to day, the more we will help others find Him and thus find their own courage. In essence, it is our duty to become a spokesperson for the Lord. Once we have gained a

---

[201] Jenkins, Carri P. "A Solemn Obligation." *BYU Speeches*, 8 Nov. 2005, speeches.byu.edu/talks/carri-p-jenkins/solemn-obligation/.

firm understanding of His love and His plan, through obedience to our baptismal covenants, we commit to taking upon us His name.

Perhaps being a spokesperson for the Lord sounds daunting. It definitely can be. But it is also rest, the Lord's rest. The rest that comes from doing what we were called to do and knowing who we truly are. There is a confidence, peace, and joy that come when we are fully engaged in our eternal mission. Jenkins exclaimed, "…do not be afraid; seek and recognize the Lord's support; prepare yourself; however, do not go beyond the bounds of your knowledge, understanding, and authority; be yourself; and never forget that actions speak louder than words."[202]

I love this. The Lord hasn't asked us to run someone else's race. We are all part of a relay team, each person having their own part to help us all cross the finish line. Thank goodness He has not asked me to be the sprinter who finishes the last leg of the race! My short legs would not hold up well against the long legs of someone who is 6'2". But He has asked me to endure. To keep holding to my faith and standing up for truth and to share the experiences I have had. And truthfully, I feel invigorated. Knowing that I am doing something worthwhile, something that is helping bring light to those around me has had a profound impact on my energy and the attitude with which I approach each day. On the hard days, when I am not sure if I will be granted my deepest desires, I can stand tall and reach for the scepter of the Lord. His mercy is always there. If we are having trouble seeing it, we can return to the foundation, which our personal reservoirs are built upon—scripture study, prayer, and journal archives of past experiences. Anything that reminds us of His love for us.

Once the king had agreed to allow the Jews to fight against their enemies, they had their own experience with this change of attitude. In Esther 9:22 we read, "As the days wherein the Jews rested from

---

[202] Ibid.

their enemies, and the month which was turned unto them from sorrow to joy, and from mourning into a good day: that they should make them days of feasting and joy, and of sending portions one to another, and gifts to the poor." The lives of an entire community completely changed because one person was willing to stand boldly. Esther knew that she could not keep her good fortune to herself. She used her newfound power and authority to influence the king for righteousness.

It is in the choosing of how we will use our discovered identity that we gain a deeper understanding of the Atonement of Jesus Christ. We can, and should, draw on the power of His Atonement to purify and heal ourselves. It is what we do after this, after we have experienced the healing power that uncovers our true nature. When Esther took a risk and confronted the king, she revealed who she really was and that she understood the responsibility she had to help those who could not help themselves. Barbara B. Smith said this of Jesus: "Day by day he made decisions so that he could be the great example of courage."[203] It is in studying Christ's life that we come to understand what Esther did, that her status and power did not determine her true nature. Her true nature was revealed when she begged the king, "…and if it please the king, let my life be given me at my petition, and my people at my request."[204]

In fact, many millennia later, through a revelation for Emma Smith, the Lord commanded her "…to expound scriptures, and to exhort the church, according as it shall be given [her] by my Spirit."[205] He was not just giving this message to Emma. The revelation concludes with verse 16, "And verily, verily, I say unto you, that this is my voice unto ALL. Amen."[206] The Lord needs us to be His mouthpiece. He knows that sometimes people cannot hear the still small voice of the

---

[203] Smith, Barbara B. " '. . . For Such a Time as This.' " *BYU Speeches*, 16 Feb. 1982, speeches.byu.edu/talks/barbara-b-smith/time/.
[204] Esther 7:3, Holy Bible, KJV.
[205] Doctrine and Covenants 25:7
[206] Doctrine and Covenants 25:16. Emphasis added.

Holy Ghost. We are all currently natural women, and our earthly bodies sometimes need tangible evidence. We need to see, feel, taste, touch, or hear via our physical bodies. The Lord uses all of His children to accomplish His great works. When a woman, working through the Spirit of the Lord, uses her words and actions to talk of Christ, those around her are blessed. How often have you heard someone say "that was exactly what I needed to hear today"? You are a spokesperson; now is the time to fulfill your role with more intention.

Being intentional about fulfilling the Lord's purpose for you does not come easy and it is a life-long process. It involves staying in close contact with the Holy Ghost and also learning to recognize all the ways the Lord speaks to you. One of the ways I have found the Lord speaks to me is repetition. I mentioned earlier that I have a child who has struggled with crippling anxiety from the time she was a preschooler. For years, I did not talk about it. I always want to respect my children and their privacy. I also do not feel like the world needs to know every trial we each face. There are definitely things we can keep between us and the Lord. The past few years, however, I repeatedly had the thought to start publicly talking about some of the things our family was going through, with my middle daughter specifically. As I have opened up, I have seen my contact list expand. I have received ideas and resources to help my daughter. I have become someone who others can trust. My daughter has learned that by her willingness to share her experiences, she can help another child find help or feel less alone. So much good has come from us speaking up about what we've learned, what has helped, or when we experience setbacks. It took repeated promptings from the Lord for me to finally understand what He was asking me to do. He knows that other people need to hear that they are not alone in their struggles with mental health challenges.

Take a minute to pause and reflect. Is there something in your life that you have had repeated thoughts about? Something that you think you should do or say? Have you written the same idea in your journal on numerous occasions? Does the same phrase or person keep showing up in random places? Chances are, if it just does not go away, the Lord may be trying to tell you something.

Maybe you are someone who feels terrified at the idea of being a spokesperson. Maybe you identify as an introvert. Maybe you do not see yourself as good enough. Maybe you are too tired to exert effort above daily tasks. Maybe you think you do not know enough people. Maybe you just have trouble getting started. I know that feeling well!

As I am growing into the discomfort of being a spokesperson, there are a few things that make it feel a little less difficult. First, just start saying "yes." My courage has grown with each "yes." Sure, I have had times where I fall back into my safe space and want to stay quiet. There are times that is where I am meant to be. But I am learning that if I stay in hermit mode too long that is where Satan wants me because,

> "It is in the choosing of how we will use our discovered identity that we gain a deeper understanding of the Atonement of Jesus Christ."
>
> - Audra Elkington

when I am not on the Lord's errand, he can more easily sway me to be on *his* self-serving errand—which is to make each of us miserable, like him. Doing the Lord's work is invigorating. It comes with a peace of mind that cannot be matched by anything or anyone else. But you have to take that first step. For me, the first "yes" was walking back into a chapel for the first time in five years. It was extremely uncomfortable, nausea-inducing to be honest. But I was sure this was the step the Lord wanted me to take.

Saying "yes" is important. Along with that, it is equally important to understand how the Lord speaks to you. Is He filling your mind with the repetitive thoughts or themes mentioned earlier? Is He opening doors that you never would have imagined would open? Do you have a friend or family member who is constantly encouraging you and reminding you what your strengths are? Do you find yourself interested in doing things that might not make sense to others? Take some time to really think about this. Get down on your knees and ask for confirmation to know if you are on the right path. Take note of your emotions and how you feel. For me, I have found daily journaling to be very helpful. There is no flow to my journal entries, it is a jumble of every single thought that enters my mind as I write each morning. They are notes that I take as I study my scriptures. I try to write down memorable quotes from people I talk to each day; if it sticks out to me, I write it down. Every couple of months, I re-read my entries and almost always see a theme. This has helped me to understand that it truly is the Lord speaking to me, which then helps me to say "yes."

Another thing that has been helpful for me is to read my patriarchal blessing on a regular basis. I went years without even knowing where mine was. In the past three years, however, I have read through it at least once a month. It has helped me to clearly see what the Lord needs me to do in that specific phase of life. This is the most personalized direction we receive from our Father in Heaven and often underutilized. Referring to patriarchal blessings, Julie B. Beck said, "When we know who we are and what we are supposed to do…it is easier to shine our light in our families, with our friends, and in all other places."[207] That is exactly what the Lord wants us to do—shine our light. Our patriarchal blessings can help us to know our strengths and gifts. It is easier to shine a light using the talents we have been blessed with.

Lastly, remember that being a spokesperson for the Lord does not necessarily look like sharing your light with large congregations or a million followers on social media or podcasting for whoever decides

---

[207] Beck, Julie B. "You Have a Noble Birthright," General Conference April 2006

to download your voice. In the General Handbook: Serving in The Church of Jesus Christ of Latter-day Saints, it outlines the purpose of the Relief Society, which is "to help women and their families come unto Christ. This means bringing the influence of Jesus Christ into our homes." We need to re-evaluate the definition of what it means to be a spokesperson. Merriam-Webster Dictionary defines a spokesperson as "a person who speaks as the representative of another." Nowhere in that definition is the audience defined. You represent Christ just by virtue of living like Him—within the walls of your home or outside of them. Think about Esther. Her audience changed throughout her story. First, she shared only with Mordecai. From there, she progressed to the maiden's home, then on to the king and his court. Once there, she proceeded to speak on behalf of all the Jews.

Perhaps right now, you are in the throes of life with small children, and all you feel capable of is teaching them that Jesus loves them. Maybe you're a college student, surrounded by those in a similar life circumstance and your calling is to stand as a witness for Christ. Or maybe you are teaching today's teenagers and hoping they feel their Savior's love through your actions. Some of you are grandmas, sharing your experiences from a life well-lived (and maybe some not so fun consequences from poor choices). And others are feeling compelled to speak out more publicly, via writing, podcasting, or speaking on stage. Whatever audience you have, the Lord will use you. He will always use the willing heart to help bring even just one person back to His presence.

Drawing your attention back to Esther, it was because of her boldness that the Jews were able to overcome their enemies and enjoy freedom. In Esther 8:16 we read, "The Jews had light, and gladness, and joy, and honor." And then in 9:16, "Jews that were in the king's provinces gathered themselves together, and stood for their lives, and had rest from their enemies." How validating this must have been for Esther. If you have had the experience of knowing you helped another person feel the love of Jesus Christ, you can probably imagine how Esther must have been feeling. If you have felt His love and know the peace it can bring you, you do not want to keep that to yourself. That feeling of rest compels us to speak out, to talk of Christ, rejoice in Christ. Carri P. Jenkins said that as disciples of Jesus Christ, "we must accept that for someone – and perhaps for a great many – we are their closest source...to the Church. Their opinions rest on our words and on our actions."[208] To some, that might feel like a heavy obligation. It does not have to be. In fact, the Lord intends for us to feel joy as we act on personal revelation and promptings of the Holy Ghost. Each time you act or speak the Spirit will confirm truths, not only to your own mind but also to the minds of those within the reach of your voice.

The more women who are willing to push past their nervousness and share their sweet testimonies, the more people will begin to turn to the Savior. One by one, we can create a community of people who are endowed with the Spirit of the Lord. When His power permeates our communities, we can live as the Jews did once they had been granted freedom—lives filled with light, happiness, and joy.

In the past few years, I have made it my personal goal to share my testimony and what I am learning about the Savior every chance I get. I have said "yes" to opportunities I would never have even given a thought to in the past. My desire to help in the gathering of Israel and bring others to know their Savior has increased exponentially. With every action completed, I feel Heavenly Father granting me an increase in courage. My own life becomes more joyful knowing that I am spending my time talking about the most important things.

Heavenly Father said in the Book of Moses, "For behold, this is my work and my glory, to bring to pass the immortality and eternal life of man."[209] The more I come to know Him, the more I want my

---

[208] Jenkins, Carri P. "A Solemn Obligation." *BYU Speeches*, 8 Nov. 2005, speeches.byu.edu/talks/carri-p-jenkins/solemn-obligation/.
[209] Moses 1:39, The Pearl of Great Price.

work to become His work. This is being a spokeswoman for the Lord. He uses the one, to bring in the one.

The more women who are willing to push past their nervousness and share their sweet testimonies, the more people will begin to turn to the Savior.

— Audra Elkington —

—6—
Lauren Madsen

Building a Legacy With the Words We Use

It is a story our family has heard over and over and it still makes me chuckle every time. Picture a five-year-old in pigtails, frantically preparing pretend pies for the upcoming barn raising (big fan of Seven Brides for Seven Brothers over here). As was typical, I was on what was likely my seventh outfit of the day, with shirts, skirts, hair bows, and shoes covering my bedroom floor. When my mom opened the door and said, "Lauren, it's time to clean up," I was instantly snapped out of my imaginary world. Frustrated at the interruption, I put my hands on my hips and declared, "Mom, I am not a girl who cleans up, I'm just not that kind of girl!"

Now, when I think of how five-year-old Lauren defined herself, I find myself pondering, "I am still not a girl who loves to clean up, but what kind of girl am I?" I am the kind of girl who tries to do the right thing and knows she has a work to do. In a world where darkness seems to be spreading in every direction, I am the kind of girl who wants to better understand and utilize the power of my words to brighten the world around me as I point others to Jesus Christ.

As women who seek to be distinct and different, we can embrace the immense power that comes from the words we think, the words we speak, and the words we write. The right words at the right time can be one of the greatest gifts we could ever give in this life and they have the potential to last far beyond here and now.

Expectations & Affirmations

In the fall of 2019, my four kids ranged in age from three to eleven. Every morning as we drove to school my kids would hear me say things like, "Why does it take you so long to get your shoes on?!" and "How many times have I told you to brush your teeth after you eat?!" and "Ugh! We need to leave at 8:55, not 9:04. How hard is it?!" and "You guys are making me CRAZY!" Perhaps these words sound familiar to you. When we would arrive at school the older kids would climb out of the car and I'd quickly tell them I loved them and to have a good day. I wondered if they believed me, that I really did love them, and wanted them to have a good day. My previous words had been spewed out in irritation and anger, so who could blame them if they didn't?

Morning after morning, I would drive back home and shudder as I thought back on the words my kids were hearing all the way to school. From MY mouth! It was not what I wanted for them. Our

Heavenly Parents wouldn't want it for them either. They had entrusted these children to me. Something had to change, so I started by asking myself what I really valued. I genuinely valued being on time. But I quickly acknowledged that I valued my kids and their hearts even more. My thoughts about being late had to stop. This wasn't easy. My whole life I've appreciated punctuality. But was leaving for school a couple of minutes late really so bad? The answer was no. It wasn't so bad and did not need to be the big deal I was making it.

Primary General President Joy D. Jones has pointed out, "It is...instructive to recognize who wants us to give in to enticements as he tempts us to become impatient, frustrated, doubtful, fearful, or angry."[210] Satan had been winning for too long and I knew it. Instead of filling my kids' ears and heads full of "why can't you just...?" or "how many times do I have to tell you?...", I decided to spend that 3-minute drive building them up. And I knew affirmations were a great place to start.

It didn't take long for me to think up some positive phrases I wanted my kids to have in their heads—simple phrases that would remind them who they are and what they are capable of. I typed up and laminated a list of affirmations for them to say out loud together on our way to school every day. "I am a Madsen. I am kind. I am strong. I am a helper. I am a friend. I solve problems. I do hard things. I try my best. I am a child of God. I am loved." I recently asked my kids if reciting these daily had any effect on them. My twelve year old responded that if she was worried about something when she got in the car, those affirmations helped her feel like everything was going to be okay. My nine year old told me that saying them helped her feel like it was going to be a good day. My

---

[210] Jones, Joy D. "Look unto Him in Every Thought." *BYU Speeches*, 21 Aug. 2018, speeches.byu.edu/talks/joy-d-jones/look-unto-him-every-thought/.

six year old told me simply, "It makes me happy." Reassurance, hope and happiness. I am calling that a win.

Choosing *different* words made our mornings *different*. It made *us* different. Yes, we have rough mornings here and there. But with a few adjustments in my mindset and in the words we choose to speak, I drop them off at school without regrets. We still make it to school on time. But now we do it with smiles.

Thoughts, Repentance & The Words We Speak

During my morning meditation routine, I ask Heavenly Father to forgive me for my mistakes and for help in my weaknesses. Some mornings I openly ask Him what it is I need to do better. The more I do this the more the Spirit reveals. It sounds overwhelming, but I have found the opposite to be true. I feel empowered in a true partnership between me and my Heavenly Parents in my attempts to become all they know I can be. I don't feel guilt or gloom, I feel ABLE—a feeling that I know comes by and through the atonement of Jesus Christ.

I remember well the morning I had this thought come to me, "You need to stop criticizing other people. Your kids are listening." It didn't take long for me to recognize that it was true. I would talk about other people in front of them. I recalled a verse in Ephesians: "Let no corrupt communication proceed out of your mouth, but that which is good to the use of edifying, that it may minister grace unto the hearers."[211] Then King Benjamin's warning to his people came to mind: "But this much I can tell you, that if ye do not watch yourselves, and your thoughts, and your words, and your deeds, and observe the commandments of God, and continue in the faith of what ye have heard concerning the coming of our Lord, even unto the end of your lives, ye must perish. And now, O man, remember, and perish not."[212] I recognized the need to watch my words and the Spirit helped me to identify the root of my problem. It was the frustration I experienced when people did not do things the way I would choose to do them. It began with my thoughts, long before they came out of my mouth. True, biting my tongue would keep the words from coming out, but I also needed to work on the words in my head. I remind myself daily that my way is not the only way. It is a constant work, a continual effort.

One of my favorite books is Pollyanna—a sweet story about an orphan girl who comes to live with her aunt in a new town. She was taught by her father from an early age to look on the bright side of things and her attitude starts to rub off on the people around her. The minister in town is touched by her outlook and, in his readings, comes across this idea: "People radiate what is in their minds and in their hearts. . . .When you look for the bad, expecting it, you will get it. When you know you will find the good—you will get that."[213] Have you experienced this? I certainly have, both inside and outside my own home. The choice is ours when we interpret what we see, and it begins with our thoughts.

> "*The right words at the right time can be one of the greatest gifts we could ever give in this life and they have the potential to last far beyond here and now.*"
> - Lauren Madsen

Christian author Sharon Jaynes asks this important question: "How will we use our words? Will we use them to defend or defeat, complete or compete, praise or put down? The choice begins in our

---

[211] Ephesians 4:29, Holy Bible, KJV.
[212] Mosiah 4:30, The Book of Mormon.
[213] Porter, Eleanor H. *Pollyanna*. eBook, Sterling Pub Co., 1913.

minds, runs through our hearts, and responds with our lips."[214] I think of Sariah in The Book of Mormon. She left everything behind—her home, her friends, all of it—to obey the Lord who told her husband to pack up his family and leave Jerusalem. When her sons were sent back to the very place they fled from and they hadn't returned, Sariah feared the worst. At one point she "complained against" Lehi.[215] When her sons eventually did make it back, she acknowledged that Lehi had indeed been commanded to leave Jerusalem and she also praised God for keeping her sons safe: "Now I know of a surety that the Lord hath commanded my husband to flee into the wilderness; yea, and I also know of a surety that the Lord hath protected my sons, and delivered them out of the hands of Laban."[216]

Here is the truth—we will not say perfect words all of the time. When emotions run high, I sometimes say things I later regret, even to the people I love the very most! The legacy I choose to leave behind will not be one of perfection, but I *will* use my words to try to make things better. We may not be able to un-say words that hurt, but we have words like "I'm sorry" and "I made a mistake" and "Please forgive me" always available. Mercifully, we always have the gift of repentance and second chances.

What about when people we love make poor choices or do things that irritate, hurt, or disappoint us? When our children, spouse, or others we love make mistakes, are we using our words to convey the love, forgiveness, and forbearance Heavenly Parents have for us? Or are we using our words to express our disapproval and impatience at others' imperfections? Elder Jeffrey R. Holland said, "Our words...should be filled with faith and hope and charity.... With such words, spoken under the influence of the Spirit, tears can be dried,

---

[214] Jaynes, Sharon. *The Power of a Woman's Words.* kindle ed., Harvest House Publishers, 2020, p.74.
[215] 1 Nephi 5:2, The Book of Mormon.

hearts can be healed, lives can be elevated, hope can return, confidence can prevail."[217] If we hope to dry tears, heal hearts, and elevate lives we have to ask for and allow the Spirit to guide us to know WHEN to speak, WHAT to speak, and HOW to speak it. We have this promise: "For it shall be given you in the very hour, yea, in the very moment, what ye shall say."[218] Author Stephanie Dibb Sorenson wrote: "Jesus Christ could literally calm troubled seas with His faith-filled voice of reassurance. Mothers, too, hold that power in their homes. Their voices, their words, their gentle touch can restore calm to troubled souls."[219]

Words of Encouragement

My paternal grandmother passed away in March 2017. She was a special lady who always seemed to know just what to say. So much about what was shared at her funeral revolved around her words. Some phrases were just so Grandma. "Don't give up the ship" and "I love you a bushel and a peck". I remember listening to my uncle, his eyes brimming with tender tears, as he recalled a letter she had written to him about her love for him and concern for his choices. This loving mother's words remained in her son's heart some forty years later. Grandma's words to me after I suffered two consecutive miscarriages brought me a comfort I still carry when things go differently than I had planned. Although I can't recall the exact words she used, I will always remember the feeling I had—being buoyed up when I felt like I was drowning. Our words can be like tossing out a life preserver to someone struggling to keep their head above water. We may not be able to stop life's storms for someone, but our words can help them survive. We can inspire. We can lift. We can save. I agree with Sharon Jaynes: "Our very words have the

---

[216] 1 Nephi 5:8, The Book of Mormon.

[217] Holland, Jeffrey R. "The Tongue of Angels," General Conference April 2007

[218] Doctrine and Covenants 100:6.

[219] Sorenson, Stephanie D. *Covenant Motherhood: Reflecting the Role of Christ in Our Lives.* eBook, Covenant Communications Inc., 2013.

potential to change the course of a day...to change the course of a life."[220]

Every few weeks I get to hop on a Zoom call with some friends from all over the United States. We discuss conference talks or BYU speeches, but before we begin, we take turns sharing what is going on in our lives. At the end of one of our calls I was deeply touched as one of these sweet women asked if she could pray with each of us. We bowed our heads, in different places across the country, and listened as she said our names and prayed specifically for the things we were struggling with or needing. This experience changed me. I have had people tell me they would pray *for* me before, but no one had ever offered to pray *with* me. Talk about real, sincere encouragement.

What if you feel prompted to encourage someone, but you don't know what to say? President Henry B. Eyring promises, "I testify that the Lord goes before your face whenever you are on His errand. Sometimes you will be the angel the Lord sends to bear others up."[221] About two years ago I had the impression to start writing letters to someone in my family who I knew could use some encouragement. I hadn't seen or talked to this person for close to fifteen years, so when the prompting came to write I dismissed it at first because I didn't know what to say. How would I even begin? I fought these feelings for a time but in the end, I decided to listen and to act.

I remember sitting at my desk, my mind as blank as the paper in front of me. With my pen in my hand, I whispered a prayer that I would write something that might benefit this family member. I hoped I could help this person feel not only my love, but God's love

---

[220] Jaynes, Sharon. *The Power of a Woman's Words*. kindle ed., Harvest House Publishers, 2020, p.232.
[221] Eyring, Henry B. "Fear Not To Do Good," General Conference October 2017

as well. With a pounding heart, I wrote what I hoped was inspiration and stuck the letter in the mailbox. Several letters have been written back and forth since that day and I can say that knowing what to write has gotten easier. My confidence in hearing the Spirit through thoughts and ideas has grown. More than once this person has thanked me for writing because my words have brought hope. In the last letter I received, this family member told me I have been an "Angel of Light."

This is what is possible when we work with Heavenly Father to bless His children. Our words become not only powerful, but heaven-sent. It is a responsibility He trusts us with and as author Roxanne Thayne attests, "If that translates into us being willing to open our mouths and God graciously filling them with the words we are to speak, then that is what we are to do. It's a two-way promise, and He never fails us."[222]

Expressing Gratitude to God & Others

In the New Testament, Paul describes to the Thessalonians several things followers of Christ should do, including this: "In every thing give thanks: for this is the will of God in Christ Jesus concerning you."[223] King Benjamin admonished his people: "O how you ought to thank your heavenly King! ...that God who has created you, and has kept and preserved you, and has caused that ye should rejoice, and has granted that ye should live in peace one with another."[224]

As part of my morning meditation, I take a minute or two to jot down a few things I am grateful for. When I am done I speak them in prayer. Even in the most trying times, when I choose to look, I can

---

[222] Thayne, Roxanne. *Jewels In Your Pocket: How to Comfortably Share Your Faith Through the Power of Personal Stories.* Rooftop Publishing, 2019.
[223] 1 Thessalonians 5:18, Holy Bible, KJV.
[224] Mosiah 2:19-20, The Book of Mormon.

see God's hand in my life. Elaine L. Jack, former Relief Society General President, described many things we can thank the Lord for, including our testimonies and the fact that we are alive, as well as thanking Him for our knowledge of Him as we go through challenges. She concluded, "We sisters in Zion have the best reasons to thank the Lord."[225]

> *"We may not be able to stop life's storms for someone, but our words can help them survive."*
> - Lauren Madsen

Do we also thank the people God sends to us in our time of need—the angels among us? We know that Heavenly Father often answers our prayers through other people[226], so when we receive blessings it often means there are at least two individuals we have the opportunity to thank. In her book, *Love Is A Verb*, author Mary Ellen Edmunds describes what she calls the "Wait-A-While Club". Members of the Club are people who often think back on those who have blessed their lives and thank them for the blessing they have been. We can thank others who have been a good example, who served us in a church calling, who gave a touching talk in sacrament meeting, who posted something online they felt inspired to share, or texted us encouraging words just when we needed them. Is there someone you meant to thank, but never got around to it? Sister Edmunds asks, "Have you waited quite a while? Are there letters you've meant to write, visits you've meant to make, phone calls on a list somewhere? Even if it's been a long, long while, it's never too late to thank someone."[227] Whether someone blessed your life a long time ago or just today, remember it is downright heart-warming to be thanked.

---

[225] Jack, Elaine L. "Look Up and Press On," Relief Society Sesquicentennial Satellite Broadcast General Conference April 1992

[226] Kimball, Spencer W. "Small Acts of Service." *The Church of Jesus Christ of Latter-Day Saints*, Dec. 1974, www.churchofjesuschrist.org/study/ensign/1974/12/small-acts-of-service?lang=eng.

[227] Edmunds, Mary E. *Love is a Verb*. eBook, Bookcraft Publishing, 2002.

There is nothing quite like getting a message from someone who says, "Thank you so much. It was just what I needed."

A Word on Social Media

So much of our communication these days happens through the written word. Texts, emails, DMs, PMs, and let's not forget the comments sections on platforms like Instagram and Facebook. Every day we hold in our hands this miraculous tool that allows us to communicate with people all over the world. I ask myself from time to time: What am I doing with this miracle?

In our current online world, it seems that in many ways manners, respect, and common courtesy have been lost. People bravely type things they might never consider saying to someone face to face. There are heated debates and polarizing issues everywhere you look. In 1989, long before cell phones and social media, Jutta Baum Busche offered this counsel at BYU Women's Conference: "Our efforts should not be to *perform* nor to *conform* but to be *transformed* by the Spirit."[228] How can we apply this to our online presence? Do we conform to the world's standards of posting, sharing, and commenting? Are our words harsh, laced with spite or sarcasm? Do we type things we wouldn't feel comfortable saying to someone in person? What if we could commit to letting the Spirit transform us and our interactions with others? Could we allow the Spirit to guide us through a comment rather than our own (sometimes intense) feelings? When we see a post we feel strongly about and would like to respond, what if we said a prayer before doing so? What if we ask for help in sharing our beliefs or opinions on whatever it is in a coherent, kind, and compassionate way?

---

[228] Busche, Jutta Baum. "I Think I'll Be Myself." *The Church of Jesus Christ of Latter-day Saints*, Sept. 2018, www.churchofjesuschrist.org/study/ensign/2018/09/i-think-ill-be-myself?lang=eng.

I remember being offended about a comment someone made on my post in our neighborhood Facebook group. My blood was boiling. I felt misunderstood and attacked and I wanted to defend myself, with a little vengefulness thrown in. Through gritted teeth, I began typing a snooty reply. Then the wise words of my husband came to mind: "What good will it do?" He had asked this question more than once in our married life, and I had used it before to evaluate my impulsive course of action. I stopped to think. Would what I was typing change this person's mind? Would any good come from it? Would it help the situation in any way? Nope. It wouldn't. I deleted my words, put the phone down, and walked away.

The Savior taught the Nephites, "For verily, verily I say unto you, he that hath the spirit of contention is not of me, but is of the devil, who is the father of contention, and he stirreth up the hearts of men to contend with anger, one with another."[229] When we allow ourselves to be stirred up, we may feel the regret over our contentious words, but I have NEVER regretted taking some time for my emotions to simmer down. Sometimes we can let things go. Sometimes we can let things sit. Sometimes we do need to take a stand. We can remember though that it's not just what we say, but how we say it that makes us distinct and different. One way can lead to understanding through respect, the other can lead to toxic comebacks and back-and-forth bickering.

I have been thinking about how the last sentence in the 13th Article of Faith applies to the things I write online, "If there is anything virtuous, lovely, or of good report or praiseworthy, we seek after these things."[230] As I am writing a response to a text, email, or post, I try to ask: Are these words virtuous, lovely, or of good report or praiseworthy? Former Young Women General President Margaret

---

[229] 3 Nephi 11:29, The Book of Mormon.
[230] "Article of Faith 13." *The Church of Jesus Christ of Latter-day Saints*, www.churchofjesuschrist.org/study/scriptures/pgp/a-of-f/1?lang=eng.

D. Nadauld taught, "The world has enough women who are tough; we need women who are tender. There are enough women who are coarse; we need women who are kind. There are enough women who are rude; we need women who are refined."[231] Let us be those tender and refined women in our online communications, shining Christlike kindness for others to see.

Stories Have Lasting Influence

Throughout the history of the Church prophets and apostles have spoken of the importance of recording our experiences —from Wilford Woodruff[232] to Spencer W. Kimball[233] and more recently President Henry B. Eyring[234] to Elder Neil L. Andersen[235]. Do you realize when you leave this world, you take with you the very thing you can also leave behind? YOUR STORIES. Each of us has experienced and is now experiencing stories of trial and triumph, sorrow and joy, despair and hope, obstacles and overcoming. Unless we record them, though, our stories will not linger very long once we are gone.

Why are stories important? What is the result of sharing a simple story? Author Roxanne Thayne wrote, "Your simple or common story can leave your listener comforted, encouraged, enlightened, emboldened, educated, motivated, reassured, validated, entertained, cheered, [and] oriented."[236] If we truly believe our words have the

---

[231] Nadauld, Margaret D. "The Joy of Womanhood," General Conference October 2000

[232] Woodruff, Wilford. "Chapter 13: Journals: Of Far More Worth than Gold," *Teachings of Presidents of the Church: Wilford Woodruff.* 2004. Intellectual Reserve, Inc., Salt Lake City, 2011. www.churchofjesuschrist.org/study/manual/teachings-wilford-woodruff/chapter-13?lang=eng.

[233] Kimball, Spencer W. "The Angels May Quote from It." *New Era,* 1974, www.churchofjesuschrist.org/study/new-era/2003/02/the-angels-may-quote-from-it?lang=eng.

[234] Eyring, Henry B. "O Remember, Remember," General Conference October 2007

[235] Andersen, Neil L. "Spiritually Defining Memories," General Conference April 2020

[236] Thayne, Roxanne. *Jewels In Your Pocket: How to Comfortably Share Your Faith Through the Power of Personal Stories.* Rooftop Publishing, 2019, p.52.

power and potential to have this kind of long-lasting influence, we must make a commitment to WRITE THEM DOWN. If inspired people through the ages had not written down their experiences with God, we would have no scriptures! I think of Nephi explaining the why of his record-keeping efforts: "For we labor diligently to write, to persuade our children, and also our brethren, to believe in Christ, and to be reconciled to God."[237] Our sacred personal histories can become like scripture for our posterity. So ask yourself—what stories will you leave behind?

I am forever grateful for my ancestors who took the time to write down stories. There is one, in particular, I think back on often that my great grandmother took the time to record. It was the story she had heard of her mother-in-law as a young mother. My great-great-grandmother Lydia Elizabeth Hopkins Jarman "often experienced personal revelation regarding her family." As the story goes, one of many such experiences happened one stormy night as her young boys were playing games around the room in their home. As the thunder clapped and the lightning flashed outside, Lydia yelled to the children, "Get away from that door!" The children quickly complied and a strong gust of wind knocked the door off its hinges, which in turn knocked a kerosene lamp off a shelf. Coal oil ran all over the floor and caught fire. Lydia quickly grabbed a quilt to smother the fire. Had the children hesitated in obeying, or had Lydia second-guessed the prompting, they could have been seriously hurt. This story has strengthened me in trusting my own promptings and my children have been blessed by hearing of the immediate obedience of their great-great-grandfather. All of this from one brief paragraph!

Many of us recognize the importance of stories, but still experience roadblocks when it comes to recording them. For some, our

---

[237] 2 Nephi 25:23, The Book of Mormon.

hesitations include: my stories are not interesting enough or I don't feel I am a very good writer. I have spent a good deal of time over the past few years perusing memories in Family Search. Never once have I read a story of an ancestor and thought, "Wow, that wasn't very well written." I also have never finished reading a story and wondered why they bothered to record it. EVERY TIME I read even one sentence, I am grateful for the tiniest glimpse into the lives of my ancestors. Through their stories, I connect with them and they become my people.

We cannot afford to question the worth of our stories. I believe the adversary is behind such thoughts because he understands well the power they hold. Elder Dieter F. Uchtdorf said, "Sometimes your stories make people laugh. Sometimes they bring them to tears. Sometimes

> "Our sacred personal histories can become like scripture for our posterity."
> - Lauren Madsen

they will help people to continue in patience, resilience, and courage to face another hour, another day and come a little closer to God."[238] The adversary wants none of those things for us and those we love, so he will try to convince you that your stories are not worth recording, or at the very least, he will tempt you to procrastinate. If each new day we say, "Someday I'll write them down," our stories will never be written.

Once we commit to recording our stories, what stories should we write? We might begin with what we want those who come after us to know. I want those who come after me to know how I came to know that God is real. I want them to know that he knows us, loves us, and blesses us in ways both big and small. When I was eight

---

[238] Uchtdorf, Dieter F. "Your Great Adventure," General Conference October 2019

years old, my grandparents came over to help my mom replace a doorknob. For some long-forgotten reason, they couldn't stay to finish the project and the old doorknob was left unscrewed and hanging from the door. My mom did everything she could think of, but the knob would not come off. She whispered a desperate prayer as the sun started to set in the sky. Being a single mom, she wanted very much to be able to lock the front door that night. As soon her prayer ended, that stubborn doorknob fell off the door right into her hands. It is a simple, faith-promoting story of an answered prayer that can and should be passed on.

Have your prayers been answered? Have you felt the reality and nearness of God? Have you experienced the power of Christ's atonement in your life? Have you suffered through pain? Despair? Loneliness? What carried you through? What fights have you fought? What passions have you pursued? Have you traveled through peaceful valleys and climbed impossible mountains and basked in the glorious views at the top? These are stories to tell. These are stories to record. These are the stories to leave behind.

YOUR Words Are Needed

As sisters in the gospel, we have great power when we choose to use our words in distinct and different ways. There are vast and varied opportunities before us in the words we choose to think, speak, and write. Every day we are placed in the paths of people who need what only we can give. Each of us has our own unique background, experiences, and gifts to help those around us feel God's love. We know we are here, now, to help prepare the world for the second coming of the Savior. Do the words we use at home, at work, at church, online, and everywhere in between reflect our discipleship? Elder M. Russell Ballard said, "The power of the voice of a converted woman is immeasurable, and the Church needs your voices now more than ever."[239] We need courageous voices to affirm and teach truth, bear testimony, and promote faith. We need voices that can encourage, uplift, and inspire. We need voices that strengthen and unify as we create a Zion-like people to whom the Savior can return.

I echo the words of Chieko N. Okazaki, former First Counselor in the Relief Society General Presidency: "Sisters, we are mighty together. There is consolation in our caring. There is strength in our sharing. There is power in our commitment to righteousness."[240] No matter where we are or who we are interacting with, let us continue on the covenant path of discipleship and strive to use our words in righteous, loving, Christlike ways.

---

[239] Ballard, M. Russell. "Let Us Think Straight." *BYU Speeches*, 20 Aug. 2013, speeches.byu.edu/talks/m-russell-ballard/let-us-think-straight-2/.
[240] Okazaki, Chieko N. "Rejoice In Every Good Thing," General Women's Meeting September 28, 1991.

*The legacy I choose
to leave behind will
not be one of
perfection, but I will
use my words to try
to make things better.*

— Lauren Madsen —

——7——
Jodi L. Nicholes

Live in Your True Identity

The sweet scent of a lilac tree immediately takes me back to my childhood. It's amazing how a particular smell or sound can conjure up a memory.

Growing up in a small farming community, I was in constant wonder and awe of life around me. During the spring months, I watched farm animals birth their babies. And when our family milking cow Bambie passed away, I cried. My mother would often point out the beauty of God in the seemingly small moments of each day, from sunlight dancing across an alfalfa field to the coo of a Mourning Dove. With each of these experiences, I learned about the cycle of life and developed an appreciation and love for nature, but most importantly, I learned about God.

Some of my most beloved memories revolve around endless summer days playing in the fields with my siblings and friends. At night we played games of kick-the-can and Oli-Oli-Oxen-Free. After games, we usually found ourselves gathered out on the trampoline gazing up at the starry sky, searching for constellations. Inevitably the conversation always led to God and his wondrous creation. I felt small and inadequate in comparison to the vastness of the universe. Could God really know me personally? I found myself asking this question often. Now and then, I would get a rush of warmth washing through my body. It was as if God was reminding me of who I was, who I am, and who I can become. Accompanied with this warm feeling came a deep sense of love and belonging. These moments were powerful but fleeting.

In some ways, I had two completely different childhood experiences. One experience full of wonderment and the other performing on stage.

Singing has always felt innately part of me, almost like breathing. I can't recall a period in my life where I wasn't singing. For me, singing is much more than a talent; it's a way of expressing the innermost parts of myself.

My mother was a singer. Her voice was rich and full of soul! When I was around the age of six, my dad came home with a fancy 8-track karaoke machine he purchased as a gift for her. I grabbed hold of the microphone and never let go. I began to get asked to sing at different community events. I enjoyed doing it and performing on stage felt natural as if I had done it many times before.

A few months after winning a local talent show, I performed at the state fair, where I represented my county in the state talent show. Mom and Dad loaded us kids in the car and we drove to Salt Lake City, Utah. As I stood backstage waiting for my turn to perform, I carefully sized up my competition. For the first time, I felt nervous. Yet, the moment I heard my introduction and the MC call my name, it was as if someone flipped on a light switch, and my fear shifted to electric energy.

Every contestant's performance was heard live through the speaker system at the fairgrounds. A man attending the fair that day happened to hear my performance. He was determined to put a face to the voice. He set out on a quest to find me. I don't remember specific details other than meeting a man who was excited about my talent and asked to speak with my parents. This interaction was the catalyst to the beginning of my music career. Within months I found myself singing and performing on the stages of Las Vegas Nevada for thousands.

At this point, because I was ten years old and too young to walk through a casino by myself, I was assigned a bodyguard who would walk me to and from the stage. I remember thinking, "If I need a bodyguard, I must be important."

This was a defining moment in my life. It was at this moment I began to attach my worth and value to the approval and validation of the outside world. Standing ovations and the applause of a crowd dictated who I was and who I wasn't. My parents didn't know the first thing about show business, and there was never any force or pressure from their side of things. They had no idea that the workings of my little ten-year-old mind were creating and building a framework on faulty ground and unrealistic expectations.

What my younger self didn't understand or fully comprehend was that I was living an illusion. My mind repetitively told itself a cycle of illusory untruths trying to convince anyone willing to listen, but especially me, that I had value. But in truth, no amount of decorative sequins, elaborate props, or stage lighting could avoid the inevitable. The nature of the "natural man"[241] consistently wants more.

Feeding an ego with an insatiable appetite is daunting. The ego is a monster of sorts that is always awaiting its next feeding. This false self, this illusion, was never satisfied. My worth had become entirely dependent on approval from the outside world. Every act and motive were a means to that end. By the time I reached my late teens and early twenties, I knew something needed to change! I longed for the rush of warmth and feelings of love and belonging I had felt years prior as a child.

I found myself much like the musk deer.

The Legend of the Musk Deer

Once there was a deer, who on a lovely spring day detected a mysterious and heavenly fragrance in the air. The aroma hinted of peace, beauty, and love. And like a whisper, it beckoned her onward. Determined to find the source, she set out to search the whole world to find it. She climbed dangerous icy mountain peaks, padded through steamy jungles, and trekked across endless desert sands. Wherever she went, the scent was there; faint, yet always near her. At the end of her life, exhausted from her endless search, she collapsed. As she fell, her horn pierced her belly, and suddenly the air was filled with the heavenly scent. As she lay there, she realized the beauty, the light, and the

---

[241] Mosiah 3:19, The Book of Mormon.

wonderful scent she had been searching for all along had been
coming from within her...[242]

The musk deer are one of the most endangered and rare species on
this planet. Musk deer produce the most expensive scent in the world
known as Kasturi (in Indian Ayurveda). This scent is produced in a
small pouch that sits in the naval area of the deer. The pouch is also
known as a musk pod.

Many of us will spend a large portion of our lives looking for
something to help us feel whole. We try to hold on to whatever we
think is sustainable and will bring us joy. We expect our spouse and
children to make us feel happy, a bigger bank account to bring us
peace, and a gym-toned tush and endless social media followers to
bring us value. In a desperate plea to stop time, we lather on beauty
creams and inject our faces with false promises hoping to bring back
our youth, or minimally to postpone the future. When these empty
promises can no longer feed our appetite (and they won't) we move
on to something new, and the cycle continues. No matter how
attractive or pleasing the proposal, time refuses to barter and
relationships or things cannot bring us peace and joy, at least not in
comparison to the kind of peace and joy found in Christ. Eventually,
we realize that mortal life is temporary and the things within it are
fleeting.

In Matthew 6:19-21 we read:

> *Lay not up for yourselves treasures upon earth, where moth and*
> *rust doth corrupt, and where thieves break through and steal:*
> *But lay up for yourselves treasures in heaven ... For where your*
> *treasure is, there will your heart be also.*

---

[242] *The Legend of the Musk Deer* as retold in Jodi's own words

Most of us live this illusion of a false self when we attach our value and worth to relationships and conform to the outside world's opinion of who and what we should be. This illusion clouds our vision and takes over our true identity. It whispers untruths that become our inner voice dictating our thought patterns. Like a chief conductor of an orchestra, this false identity directs our motives and actions into a daily rhythm that eventually leads to our eternal destiny.

The good news is that each of us, at one point in time, will have a life-altering event, if not many. If we allow it, these life events can shake us from our false illusions and rhythms, such as: death of a loved one, broken friendships, chronic illness, divorce, financial ruin, the birth of a baby, marriage, and love. Each opportunity, whether perceived as a trial or joyous occasion, comes with a seed for growth; and if nurtured, this seed will grow, and we will begin to see ourselves and others *as we really are*. We realize the sweet Heavenly fragrance, and the spark of the divine we've been searching for has been within us all along.

In Doctrine and Covenants 84:45-46 we find:

> *The Spirit of Jesus Christ ... giveth light to every man that cometh into the world; and the Spirit enlighteneth every man through the world, that hearkeneth to the voice of the Spirit.*

Rosemary M. Wixom has said:

> *Heavenly Father generously shares a portion of His divinity within us. That divine nature comes as a gift from Him... We*

come to this earth to nurture and discover the seeds of divine nature that are within us.[243]

True Identity versus False Identity

What are the different attributes and characteristics between our divine nature and our carnal nature?

False Identity

When we live in our false identity, we are full of selfishness, pride, envy, deceit, fear, resentment, shame, manipulation, and unhealthy levels of perfectionism. We feel worthless, unworthy, jealous, anxious, bitter, guilty, unlovable, and invisible. We see others as competitors or as a means to get something we desire. We might see ourselves below others or place ourselves above others. We see our value in terms of worldly standards. We see labels.

Natural, or carnal, men and women are without God in the world.

"And now, my son, all men that are in a state of nature, or I would say, in a carnal state, are in the gall of bitterness and in the bonds of iniquity; they are without God in the world, and they have gone contrary to the nature of God; therefore, they are in a state contrary to the nature of happiness."[244]

Living in our false self, we arrange all our goals, dreams, and plans to bring forth an outcome we desire. This is to build up our ego, to maintain the illusion that we are "somebody." Whether that

---

[243] Wixom, Rosemary M. "Discovering the Divinity Within," General Conference October 2015
[244] Alma 41:11, The Book of Mormon.

somebody is a victim or a victor, it doesn't really matter. Either way, it feeds the false self.

We live to "Eat, drink, and be merry; for tomorrow we die; and if it so be that we are guilty, God will beat us with a few stripes, and at last we shall be saved in the kingdom of God."[245]

> "Each opportunity, whether perceived as a trial or joyous occasion, comes with a seed for growth..."
>
> - Jodi Lee Nicholes

While in a carnal mindset, our worth is determined by outside influences and worldly ideals. Our false self believes that our worth comes from external factors like material possessions, our performance level, our physical appearance, or holding high-profile positions in the church. Other common wrong sources of false worth are talents, level of perceived spiritual worthiness, intelligence, and relationships. We worship these false idols hoping to find happiness, but we eventually find ourselves in a downward spiral of misery.

Our divine nature has nothing to do with our personal accomplishments, the status we achieve, the number of marathons we run, or our popularity and self-esteem. Our divine nature comes from God. It was established in an existence that preceded our birth and will continue on into eternity.[246]

---

[245] 2 Nephi 28:8, The Book of Mormon.; see also Maxwell, Neal A. "Put Off the Natural Man and Come Off Conqueror," General Conference October 1990

[246] Wixom, Rosemary M. "Discovering the Divinity Within," General Conference October 2015

Satan knows he can't progress as we do. Thus, he will do all he can in his power to try and halt our progression. He wants us to be miserable just like him. He is ruthless, sneaky, and conniving.

I've seen many women (and girls) fail to understand the difference between "worthy" and "worth" and get caught up in a deep cycle of shame. *One letter* makes all the difference.

Our culture has made it a bit confusing. When we understand and know the difference between "worthy" and "worth," it changes *everything* and can help prevent toxic shame.

To be "worthy" is to follow a specific level of obedience to the gospel of Jesus Christ that allows members to participate in different activities and ordinances and progress spiritually. It's a conditional state of being. It is a condition we strive daily to maintain or even improve. It's not to be confused with perfection but is a progression. The desired goal is to live a life equal to our inherent "worth."

Dieter F. Uchtdorf reminds us that, "Walking the path of discipleship takes practice—each day, little by little, 'grace for grace,' 'line upon line.' Sometimes two steps forward and one step back."[247]

"Worth," on the other hand, is something we already possess. As the offspring of Heavenly Parents, we brought our worth with us. It is inherent and unchanging. It is part of our eternal identity. Joy D. Jones said: "If we sin, we are less worthy, but we are never worth less!"[248]

[247] Uchtdorf, Dieter F. "Missionary Work: Sharing What Is in Your Heart," General Conference April 2019
[248] Jones, Joy D. "Value Beyond Measure", *Ensign*, November 2014, p.14.

Satan, the Adversary, can show up in many different forms. His cunning lies can begin as a simple thought that, when repeated over and over in our minds and hearts, can become a habit of belief. Dieter F. Uchtdorf has warned that "Satan might even misuse words from the scriptures that emphasize the justice of God, in order to imply that there is no mercy."[249]

When we live in our false identity, we tend to see things as black and white. If we're not perfect, then we are worthless! Tad R. Callister reminds us that: "Perfection is a quest on both sides of the veil."[250] Expecting perfection in the here and now is unrealistic and detrimental to our growth. We are spirit beings continuously evolving. Wherefore, "continue in patience until ye are perfected."[251]

When we are living in our false self, we create a bias toward ourselves and others. We no longer see other women as our sisters in God; we see them as competition. Studies show that within seconds of meeting another person, we decide all sorts of things about them, from status to intelligence. Psychologists call it "thin-slicing."[252]

The world thrives on comparing gifts, talents, and performance abilities. Just look at the many popular TV shows that rank people according to their skills and talents. "When we seek to 'complete' rather than 'compete', it is so much easier to cheer each other on!"[253] The Apostle Paul warned that people "comparing themselves among themselves, are not wise."[254]

---

[249] Uchtdorf, Dieter F. "Point of Safe Return," *Ensign*, May 2007, p.99.
[250] Callister, Tad R. "Our Identity and Our Destiny." *BYU Speeches*, 14 Aug. 2012, speeches.byu.edu/talks/tad-r-callister/our-identity-and-our-destiny/.
[251] Doctrine and Covenants 67:13
[252] Lebowitz, Shana, et al. "12 Things People Decide within Seconds of Meeting You." *Business Insider*, 10 Feb. 2020, www.businessinsider.com/things-people-decide-about-you-in-seconds-2016-11.
[253] Burton, Linda K. "We'll Ascend Together," General Conference April 2015
[254] 2 Corinthians 10:12, Holy Bible, KJV.

Don't allow yourself to get caught up in the comparison game. The second you conform to the illusion—the natural man's idea of who you should be—is the moment you lose your *special magic*! You are designed to be the best version of yourself, a literal child of God, not a knockoff version of someone else.

When we feel we aren't measuring up, we typically do one of two things: we overcompensate for our feeling of lack, or we hide away and play the victim. Playing the victim is a form of self-deprecation, which is denying the spark of divinity within us. This brings us into opposition against God.

One day when we look back over our lives, I think we'll come to understand our most significant acts of bravery and accomplishments were to show up, despite our imperfections and broken pieces. It's in the act of showing up that we are perfected.

God understands we are imperfect in our humanness. All He asks is that we try, show up, and help lift, love, and strengthen one another to become one in Christ!

God needs YOU and the unique gifts that only you can offer. Don't allow feelings of inadequacy to keep you from sharing yourself. We are all His hands.

True Identity

When we live in our true identity, we are full of mercy, charity, humility, truth, divine power, faith, knowledge, patience, obedience, compassion, gratitude, service, and empathy. We feel peace, joy, love, confidence, hope, optimism, forgiveness, and more than that, we feel whole. We see ourselves and others as children of God. We recognize others' gifts, talents, and strengths, and we desire to celebrate them. We see our worth as inherent and unchanging.

Our true self, our divine identity, was created long before we came to earth. Abraham said, "Now the Lord had shown unto me, Abraham, the intelligences that were organized before the world was; and among all these ... were many of the noble and great ones."[255]

Abraham was talking about you and me.

When we are living in our true identity, we know that we are spirit beings of light inside our body of flesh. "I am God; I made the world, and men before they were in the flesh."[256] "For I, the Lord God, created all things, of which I have spoken, spiritually, before they were naturally upon the face of the earth."[257]

We are created in the image of God. The Family: A Proclamation to the World teaches that each one of us "is a beloved spirit son or daughter of heavenly parents" and "each has a divine nature and destiny."[258]

The Apostle Paul reminds us that "we are the offspring of God,"[259] and that "we are the children of God: and if children, then heirs; heirs of God, and joint-heirs with Christ."[260] But we are much more than just spirit creations of God. We are literally His spirit children, and because we have a spark of divinity within us, we have inherited

---

[255] Abraham 3:22, The Pearl of Great Price.
[256] Moses 6:51, The Pearl of Great Price.
[257] Moses 3:5, The Pearl of Great Price.
[258] *The Family Proclamation*, Intellectual Reserve, Inc., September 1995, www.churchofjesuschrist.org/study/scriptures/the-family-a-proclamation-to-the-world/the-family-a-proclamation-to-the-world?lang=eng.
[259] Acts 17:29, Holy Bible, KJV.

spiritual traits, providing us the opportunity to become like our Father in Heaven.

Elaine L. Jack has taught: "You've inherited the characteristics of love, forgiveness, patience, service, tolerance, obedience. Christ is our example. If you wonder about other traits you have inherited, your patriarchal blessing will help you discover individual qualities."[261]

Elaine S. Dalton said: "You are set apart. You distinguished yourselves in the premortal existence. Your lineage carries with it a covenant and promises. You have inherited the spiritual attributes of the faithful."[262]

Our Savior will give us the courage to lead and share our light. As we draw closer to Him, we will find that our divine attributes are strengthened, causing us to rise to the divine potential within us.

As offspring of Heavenly parents, our worth is intrinsic and provided to us by God. It cannot be decreased. It is unchanging. In Doctrine and Covenants 18:10–11 the Lord reminds us of our value and worth to Him when He says: "Remember the worth of souls is great in the sight of God." When it comes to our divine identity (our true self), worthlessness is not an option for anyone. We are told that "the Lord seeth not as man seeth; for man looketh on the outward appearance, but the Lord looketh on the heart."[263]

When we live in our True Identity, we know that when someone else is good at something, it doesn't make *us* any less good at it. We have

---

[260] Romans 8:16-17, Holy Bible, KJV.
[261] Jack, Elaine L. "Identity of a Young Woman," *Women's Session*, General Conference October 1989
[262] Dalton, Elaine S. "It Shows in Your Face," General Conference April 2006

no desire to compete with others. Our only competition is with ourselves and our desire to live more fully in Christ. We know that what we do (sing, dance, work) and our relationships (mother, sister, friend, wife) are not who we are. We find confidence in the fact that we already have something to offer just by being ourselves. We know that, as our fingerprint, we are unique. We are unique in the way we move, stand, turn our heads, laugh, and love others.

A few years ago, my then twelve-year-old daughter wandered into the kitchen and with a concerned look on her face, asked the question: "Mom, why do girls compare the worst part of themselves to the best parts of their friend?" Not yet tainted by the world's perceptions, she wisely then added, "I don't understand; we all have amazing gifts to offer." My daughter was able to see others as they really are, each with talents, gifts, and unique personalities.

Mother Teresa's philosophy is often paraphrased with the quote, "I can do things you cannot; you can do things I cannot; together, we can do great things."[264]

Chieko N. Okazaki said: "We are literally all spiritual sisters. Each [meeting] should be a gathering of sisters who cherish each other, not choosing some to keep and throwing some back. All of us are worth keeping."[265] Sister Okazaki's words not only apply to our Latter-day Saint Relief Society sisters but all our sisters and brothers of the human race. We are, in truth, just walking each other home.

Bruce R. McConkie taught: "All the spirits of men, while yet in the Eternal Presence, developed aptitudes, talents, capacities, and abilities of every sort, kind, and degree. When we pass from

---

[263] 1 Samuel 16:7, Holy Bible, KJV.
[264] *credit given to Mother Teresa for this quote, but no documentation found of the actual quote
[265] Okazaki, Chieko N. "A Living Network," General Conference October 1995

preexistence to mortality, we bring with us the traits and talents there developed."[266]

Doctrine and Covenants 46:11-12 further states: "To some is given one, and to some is given another, that all may be profited thereby."

The gifts and talents we developed in the premortal world can play a role in our mortal existence. When we unite our gifts and talents as sisters in God, we experience miracles.

Here is a poem I wrote called Autumn Leaves:

The splendor of the autumn leaves
In golds and scarlet aflame
Each unique and different
No two are just the same
One by one they are admired
But together when they unite
The world stops in awe and wonder
to view the magnificent sight

Silvia H. Allred said: "...each of us has a vital role as a daughter of God. He has bestowed upon His daughter's divine attributes to forward His work. Our gifts, talents, skills, and spiritual strengths are greatly needed in building up the kingdom."[267]

Spend time nurturing your gifts and talents, not comparing them to others. God has a specific purpose and work for you to do. That work will look different for everyone, and it's always evolving. For some, fulfilling your purpose might require you to be in a high-

---

[266] McConkie, Bruce R. "Talents, Traits Developed in the Premortal Life Carried into Mortality." *Church News*, 13 Aug. 1994, www.thechurchnews.com/archives/1994-08-13/talents-traits-developed-in-the-premortal-life-carried-into-mortality-139191.
[267] Allred, Sylvia H. "Steadfast and Immovable," General Conference October 2010

profile position for a time; for others, you may find yourself behind the scenes in a supportive position. It's not the position but the fulfilling and accomplishing of God's work that matters, and that we thereby become all that we are designed to become in the process.

In Doctrine and Covenants 82:18 it says: "And all this for the benefit of the church of the living God, that every man may improve upon his talents."

This is a job that requires all of us.

So, how do you know if you are living in your false identity more than your true identity?

Here are a few questions to ask yourself:

> Do you ever have feelings of worthlessness, jealousy, and worry despite knowing you are a beloved daughter of Heavenly Parents?

> Do you ever feel you don't belong, and you simply can't measure up?

> Do you ever harshly judge others and yourself?

If you are human, then more than likely you answered "yes." The adversary will do all he can to keep us living in our false identity.

The Unseen Battle

I am not sure that we can fully understand the relentless efforts of the adversary. Peter said, "Be sober, be vigilant; because your adversary the devil, as a roaring lion, walketh about, seeking whom he may devour."[268] In premortality, Satan was called Lucifer, which means the "light-bearer."[269] An interesting name for someone who encompasses darkness and evil. The scriptures teach that Satan was "an angel of God who was in authority in the presence of God"[270] before he fell.

I have often wondered how a spirit with as much experience and knowledge as Lucifer could fall so far? It came down to pride! Lucifer wanted God's role and kingdom for himself, without passing through God's plan of happiness, so he rebelled.

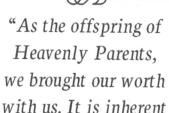

> *"As the offspring of Heavenly Parents, we brought our worth with us. It is inherent and unchanging."*
>
> *- Jodi Lee Nicholes*

A few years ago, I was visiting with an older sister in my ward who became aware of a situation between another ward member and me. The situation had become so toxic that I had no alternative but to take legal action. I was devastated! This wise older sister said something that pierced my soul, and I have never forgotten. "Jodi, I consider you to be the elite, and the adversary isn't going to do just any old thing to capture your soul. He's going to try and get you through the actions of the lady who sits a few rows behind you in your church congregation. His efforts to capture the best are going to take place within the walls of the church, among its members."

The scriptures teach that Satan "maketh war with the saints of God, and encompasseth them round about."[271] I was prayerful as I

---

[268] 1 Peter 5:8, Holy Bible, KJV.
[269] "Lucifer." *Guide to the Scriptures*, Church of Jesus Christ of Latter-day Saints, www.churchofjesuschrist.org/study/scriptures/gs/lucifer?lang=eng.
[270] Doctrine and Covenants 76:25.
[271] Doctrine and Covenants 76:29.

proceeded with legal action. It was important that I resolve the issue with the Lord's will in mind, and pay close attention to pride, as it is multifaceted and can show up in different ways. This can include an unwillingness to forgive and forms of self-deprecation and playing the victim. This was a humbling experience for me.

King Benjamin shares the following words from God with his people.

> *And finally, I cannot tell you all the things whereby ye may commit sin; for there are divers ways and means, even so many that I cannot number them. But this much I can tell you, that if ye do not watch yourselves, and your thoughts, and your words, and your deeds, and observe the commandments of God, and continue in the faith of what ye have heard concerning the coming of our Lord, even unto the end of your lives, ye must perish. And now, O man, remember, and perish not.*[272]

In 2 Nephi 28:19–23, we learn a few ways the adversary works. He grasps, pacifies, rages, stirs up, lulls, cheats, and lies. Satan is the great deceiver. Usually, his tactics are subtle. I believe one of his greatest tactics is to influence our thoughts through temptations and enticements, slowly lulling us into a seductive, hypnotic rhythm of limiting beliefs.

Science is finally catching up with doctrine on the topic of thought patterns and belief systems. "As [a man] thinketh in his heart, so is he."[273]

Over the last few decades, scientific research and analysis have uncovered the same truth the Lord revealed to Joseph Smith,[274] that

---

[272] Mosiah 4:29-30, The Book of Mormon.
[273] Proverbs 23:7, Holy Bible, KJV.
[274] Doctrine and Covenants 68:25, 27.

children come into consciousness at the age of eight. Consciousness implies the capacity to self-evaluate and realize the ability to choose to act, rather than to be acted upon, or merely to download information from external sources. Our doctrine teaches us that age eight is the age where accountability begins.

During the age of eight until adulthood, children are still susceptible to new information. Beliefs, behaviors, and habits are fresh and not fully integrated into their sense of identity yet. Add in the influence of educators, friends, and media. The more consistent these children act upon these beliefs, habits, and thought patterns, and practice them, the more they become part of their sense of self.

By looking at the brainwave patterns of newborns, toddlers, and children, scientists can help us better understand why we do the things we don't want to do. For example, a child's programming years are between the ages of 0-7. During these programming years, a child spends most of their time in Delta and Theta brainwave cycles. Delta and Theta brain frequencies are known as a hypnosis trance. In this *theta* state, children can mix the imaginary world with the real world. They are full of wonderment believing in the tooth fairy and Santa Clause. They have not yet come into a state of complete awareness.[275] This is the same neural state that hypnotherapists use to download new behaviors into the subconscious minds of their clients. A child's brain is recording all their sensory experiences and more. Like a computer program, a child is downloading enormous amounts of information about the world and the people in it. Because a child doesn't possess *full* consciousness yet, all information bypasses conscious filtration and goes directly into a child's subconscious mind.

---

[275] Kruizinga, Hendrik. "Your 5 Brainwaves: Delta, Theta, Alpha, Beta and Gamma." *Lucid*, 16 June 2016, lucid.me/blog/5-brainwaves-delta-theta-alpha-beta-gamma/.

It's important to note that the subconscious mind has no filters or bias but is designed to download anything and everything. During this time, a child learns behavioral patterns by observing those they spend the most time with. Primarily parents, caretakers, siblings, and relatives. It's through this process that children learn to distinguish acceptable and unacceptable social behaviors. Perceptions acquired from ages 0-7 become the fundamental subconscious framework that shapes the character of our lives. After the age of about 6, until the age of 8, a child will slowly start to step into full consciousness.

In my years of working with women and young girls, I have seen how a faulty framework, such as attaching value to untruths, leads to shame and despair. I find it interesting that a girl's self-esteem peaks at the age of 9, only one year after coming into a conscious brain wave pattern.

Once this framework is established, our brains begin to practice confirmation bias, favoring information that confirms our beliefs and discrediting anything that states otherwise, even with proof. These thinking errors influence how we interpret and recall information and how we see others, ourselves, and the world around us.

These narratives that are created from our framework dictate our thought patterns, which lead to our feelings, then our behavior, and ultimately our consequences.

Here's an example. Maybe you struggled to read when you were younger. A teacher or parent commented with something like, "You're nine years old you should know how to read already." Although no one told you you were stupid, you processed it that way. When you realize, almost all of the kids in your class can read, and you can't your belief that you are stupid is reinforced. You discredit anytime you do well on a test, telling yourself it was just luck. Now, as an adult, you live paycheck to paycheck, you have no college education, and you find yourself a victim of your circumstances. You tell yourself, "Nothing seems to ever work out for me."

Here's another example, let's say you overhear your older sister talking about a big date she has. You listen as she shares details about the boy who asked her out and how much happier she'll be if she can just lose 10 pounds before her big date. In your young mind, the equation is simple: Being Thin equals Love and Happiness. This belief is reinforced when the movies and commercials you see show a beautiful thin girl getting the guy. Now, as an adult, you find yourself overwhelmed and exhausted. Despite losing weight, you still aren't happy. And who has time for love? It's all you can do to get out of bed each day.

Scientist Dr. Bruce H. Lipton, Ph.D., explains that we have two separate minds.[276] There is a conscious mind that can create new ideas and think freely. Then there is the subconscious mind, which is like a computer loaded with a database of programmed behaviors. Most of these programmed behaviors were acquired before we reached the age of seven.

Our subconscious mind automatically reacts to situations, basing these reactions on previously stored behavior responses. The tricky part is that the process works without the control or knowledge or the conscious mind. This is why we are unaware of our behavior. Our subconscious mind makes everything we do and say fit a pattern that is uniform with our self-concept and belief system. Its job is to produce results. For the most part, we have no idea we are acting unconsciously.

---

[276] Lipton, Bruce. "The Jump From Cell Culture to Consciousness." *Integrative Medicine (Encinitas, Calif.)*, InnoVision Health Media Inc., Dec. 2017, pp. 44-50. Retrieved from www.ncbi.nlm.nih.gov/pmc/articles/PMC6438088/.

According to neuroscientists, the unconscious mind, also known as the "autopilot" mind, runs over 95% of our decisions, emotions, actions, and behavior.[277]

Perhaps you look in the mirror and tell yourself that you are a daughter of Heavenly Parents, but your feelings don't match that belief. You ask yourself: "Why do I feel worthless?" Now you know why! The idea of being worthless was somehow programmed into your subconscious mind, perhaps before you were eight years old.

These statistics provide insight as to how our unconscious programming shapes our reality. So, if you have unhealthy, negative programming, which almost everyone does, Dr. Lipton suggests that 95% of the time, you will recreate those negative experiences in your life.[278] And if you have ever taken the time to check out your unconscious thoughts, then you will realize that most of the programs running come from your false self.

The good news is these faulty programs can be reprogrammed. Overcoming our false self is part of God's plan.

Dual Natures and the Fall

The Fall of Adam and Eve is momentous as it pertains to the growth of our eternal destiny. With the Fall came the birth of our carnal nature. When Adam and Eve were in the Garden of Eden, they lived in a state of innocence. However, Tad R. Callister has taught that "innocence and perfection are not the same... An infant may be

---

[277] Ayan, Steve. *The Brain's Autopilot Mechanism Steers Consciousness.* 18 Dec. 2008, www.scientificamerican.com/article/the-brains-autopilot-mechanism- steers-consciousness/.

[278] Lipton, Bruce. "The Jump From Cell Culture to Consciousness." *Integrative Medicine (Encinitas, Calif.),* InnoVision Health Media Inc., Dec. 2017, pp. 44-50. Retrieved from www.ncbi.nlm.nih.gov/pmc/articles/PMC6438088/.

innocent but certainly not perfect in the sense that he or she has acquired all the attributes of godliness."[279] The scriptures corroborate this statement with 2 Nephi 2:23: "Wherefore they would have remained in a state of innocence, having no joy, for they knew no misery; doing no good, for they knew no sin."

When Adam and Eve were cast out of the Garden of Eden, they traded their state of innocence for the knowledge of good and evil. Tad R. Callister uses the metaphor of gears on a car to describe Adam and Eve's dilemma. For example, if you were invited to drive in neutral to get to your destination, you might say it's not possible. Pressing harder on the gas pedal, or "putting the pedal to the metal"[280] won't work either. Right? Tad said: "You might respond, 'That would make no difference. I cannot reach your my destination until I put my car in gear.'"[281]

So it was with Adam and Eve. They were in a state of spiritual neutrality and could not progress toward their divine destiny until they were cast out of the garden and thus put in spiritual gear.[282]

When we understand the fall of Adam and Eve, it helps bring clarity as to why dual natures are essential to Heavenly Father's plan and our eternal progression. For "it must needs be, that there is an opposition in all things. If not so ... righteousness could not be brought to pass, neither wickedness, neither holiness nor misery, neither good nor bad."[283]

---

[279] Callister, Tad R. "Our Identity and Our Destiny." *BYU Speeches*, 14 Aug. 2012, speeches.byu.edu/talks/tad-r-callister/our-identity-and-our-destiny/.

[280] Ibid.

[281] Ibid.

[282] Ibid.

[283] 2 Nephi 2:11, The Book of Mormon.

David O. McKay said: "Each of us has two contrasting natures: the physical and the spiritual. Man is a dual being."[284]

There is a conflict that comes from living with two natures. We are the offspring of God with the potential to be "partakers of the divine nature."[285] And on the other hand, because of the fall, "we are unworthy before [God]."[286] Through our agency, we decide which of these desires and passions we feed. Do we give in to the illusion, the false self, and negative thoughts, or do we nurture our divine nature and live in Christ? The scriptures teach: "No man can serve two masters: for either he will hate the one, and love the other; or else he will hold to the one, and despise the other. Ye cannot serve God and mammon."[287]

King Benjamin teaches us that "the natural man is an enemy to God, and has been from the fall of Adam."[288] He warned that in this fallen, natural state, each person will be an enemy to God forever "unless he yields to the enticings of the Holy Spirit, and putteth off the natural man and becometh a saint through the atonement of Christ the Lord."[289]

Yet, Lehi taught, "Man [can] not act for himself save it should be that he [is] enticed by the one or the other."[290] Agency demands that neither the Holy Spirit nor the evil spirit has the power to control us against our will. We must choose which enticement to follow.

---

[284] McKay, David O. *Teachings of the Presidents of the Church: David O. McKay.* 2003. Intellectual Reserve, Inc., Salt Lake City, 2011, p. 13.

[285] 2 Peter 1:4, Holy Bible, KJV.

[286] Ether 3:2, The Book of Mormon.

[287] Matthew 6:24, Holy Bible, KJV.

[288] Mosiah 3:19, The Book of Mormon.

[289] Ibid.

[290] 2 Nephi 2:16, The Book of Mormon.

From scripture we learn that no "unclean thing can enter into the kingdom of God,"[291] that because each of us sins we will all "come short of the glory of God,"[292] and that as we are, we are unworthy to return home to God's presence. This is where hope comes alive in Christ. Through His foreordained sacrifice, the plan of mercy relieves the demands of justice, and an entrance into His everlasting kingdom[293] is accessible to us.

The Gift

Living in a mortal world with competing natures can feel daunting at times. Grace is a gift from our Heavenly Father given through Jesus Christ. The word grace means "enabling power." It is the *only* power that can help us *overcome* and *become* all we are meant to be.

When my youngest child was four years old, he was anxiously counting down the days until Christmas. One morning he came to me and, in a firm voice, said, "I need Santa to come wight now!" I could tell he was frustrated. I wrapped my arms around him and reassured him that Santa would be here in a few short days. He looked at me, and with a big sigh, said, "Well, I can't wait any wonger. It's weally hawd to be dis good for dis long, mama!"

How many of us find ourselves like a child anxiously awaiting Christmas morning, in hopes that our efforts might be rewarded, that somehow we might be found worthy enough to qualify and receive the beautifully wrapped gifts under the Christmas tree? If we find ourselves in such a predicament, we are sadly missing the point. The battle to overcome our false self is not to receive an award, a fancy gift, or a prize at some future date. Salvation, and the peace it brings,

---

[291] 1 Nephi 15:34, The Book of Mormon.
[292] Romans 3:23, Holy Bible, KJV.
[293] 2 Peter 1:11, Holy Bible, KJV.

starts now! Christ is the Lord of the living, and living takes place not in the past or the future but in the present. When we are sufficiently 'Living in Christ,' the process of living within Him does the saving. As the Lord said, "He that findeth his life shall lose it: and he that loseth his life for my sake shall find it."[294]

> "Christ is the Lord of the living, and living takes place not in the past or the future but in the present."
>
> - Jodi Lee Nicholes

Grace is not something to save up and stash away. It is not a gift given on Christmas morning. It is the enabling power throughout. To try and overcome our false self through pure willpower and grit will always be insufficient. Without grace, religion and covenant-keeping feel burdensome and guilt-ridden, and we become like the impatient child, frustrated and overwhelmed, waiting for Christmas morning.

Think of it this way: Christ brings the gift to us. We still have to put in the work, but having the gift throughout the process allows us to not only enjoy Christmas day but to see and experience the magic and wonderment of the entire season, despite how difficult or hard it might be. It changes our very nature. That's how we make it through.

In November of 2012, my sister unexpectedly and tragically passed away. Our hearts were shattered into a million pieces. As the holidays approached, I found myself in a whirlwind of deep despair, reminiscing about childhood Christmases spent with my sister. I came to peace with the idea that the holidays would now stand as a

---

[294] Matthew 10:39, Holy Bible, KJV.

reminder of her tragic death. "It is, what it is," I said, and then told myself I simply had to accept it: Christmas would never be the same. And, indeed, Christmas has *not* been the same, but not in the way I had originally anticipated. I found myself celebrating my sister's *life* rather than her death. The twinkling lights on the Christmas tree are no longer just lights, and memories made with family and friends have become my greatest treasures. For the first time, I understood, on levels more profound than I had before, that the Christ child was born to die. Because of Him, my sister will live again. This new found strength and discernment came through grace. I still have moments of despair, but I'm no longer *in* despair. Grace doesn't require perfection, but progression and a sincere desire to keep trying. We will always have imperfections and broken pieces to offer up. Christ takes us as we are because perfect people don't need a Savior.

Divine Sanctification: The Antidote

What if I told you I have the recipe to help you work through doubt, fear, shame, and envy? What if it really *is* possible to have joy and genuine confidence right now? I'm here to tell you *it is possible!* This doesn't mean you won't have negative thoughts again, or that you'll never have self-doubt. What this means is that those thoughts and feelings will no longer stick and become thought patterns that dictate your life.

As we cultivate our divine nature and live in our true identity, our false self begins to lose its luster and shine. What many of us do not consider is that cultivating our divine nature is, in fact, part of our conversion to the gospel of Jesus Christ. You cannot have one without the other. They are inseparable! To know of our worth and live in our divine identity is not a one-time event but rather is something we spend a lifetime cultivating.

153

You might be surprised to learn that the recipe I am about to share is something most of you are already doing. But you may be missing crucial ingredients, which are consistency, intent, and meditative mindfulness.

The magic recipe is keeping the promises you made at baptism. These covenants are renewed during the most sacred experience of each week, the sacrament. There is a reason the sacrament is the *only* ordinance in which we make personal covenants repeatedly. It's to help us remember *who He is and who we are*. As neuroscience has taught us, our happiness and ability to navigate through life ultimately depends on our thoughts. They become what we believe, and our feelings, decisions, and our actions are a result of these thoughts. "What we love determines what we seek. What we seek determines what we think and do. What we think and do determines who we are—and who we will become."[295]

Each week we make an oath to take upon us Christ's name, mourn with those that mourn, and comfort those in need of comfort. We promise to remember him always and serve and keep his commandments.

The Apostle Paul tells us: "Know ye not, that so many of us as were baptized into Jesus Christ were baptized into his death."[296] Paul is teaching us that at baptism and each week after when we renew these same covenants, we are offering up our broken pieces, a part of our false self. We are committing to do our best to bury those pieces. Then Paul goes on to say that after our baptism we should begin a new life.[297]

---

[295] Uchtdorf, Dieter F. "The Love of God," General Conference October 2009
[296] Romans 6:3-11, Holy Bible, KJV.
[297] Romans 6:4, Holy Bible, KJV.

This is where we are born again in Christ striving to become a "new creature."[298] "Therefore, if any man be in Christ, he is a new creature: old things are passed away; behold, all things are become new."[299]

When we continue this process with real intent and consistency, we develop a pattern of divine sanctification. This divine pattern invites the Holy Ghost to live in us, direct us, and to empower us—bringing us closer to Christ, our Heavenly Father, and our divine identity. With increased purity comes heavenly eyesight, and with heavenly eyesight comes motivation and a desire to have Christ written in our hearts. Our focus shifts from living the law for the reward itself, to living in Christ. This is what it means to take upon us the name of Christ. With heavenly eyesight, we begin to see "things as they really are."[300]

Our senses tap into a hypnotic rhythm of godliness. We no longer see our children as "ours" or people as just "people." We see them as the offspring of God, divine beings with a purpose. We recognize each person as an individual spirit with a divine intelligence that was developed long before this earth. We are blessed with patience for ourselves and others with an understanding that each of us is given the challenges and growth we need to return home. Elder Neal A. Maxwell taught, "To those who have eyes to see and ears to hear, it is clear that the Father and the Son are giving away the secrets of the universe!"[301]

Living in this new rhythm of godliness, we find our senses have come alive and are enlightened. Our covenant to promise to

---

[298] 2 Corinthians 5:17, Holy Bible, KJV.
[299] Ibid.
[300] Jacob 4:13, The Book of Mormon.
[301] Maxwell, Neal A. "'Meek and Lowly.'" *BYU Speeches*, 21 Oct. 1986, speeches.byu.edu/talks/neal-a-maxwell/meek-lowly/.

"remember Him always" becomes much more than a remembrance. It's a deep mindful awareness, a constant prayer that God is in all things.[302]

Everything we see, smell, taste, and hear are reminders of Him. Each blade of grass, breath of air, and song of a bird is permeated with the goodness of God's light. We become as little children with reverence and humility, understanding that everything we are is from God.[303] The past and future no longer hold us hostage, and the present becomes magic.

We hear the ticking of the clock on the wall. We breathe in the smell of our freshly bathed toddler. We notice the chubby dimples in his or her hand as we walk together. The seemingly small moments in each day carry within them the beauty that helps mend our broken pieces. It's in these moments, God whispers, I hear you, I see you and you are loved. This is what it feels like and looks like to live in Christ. This is what it is to live in our true identity. We find we have confidence, the likes of which we've never experienced before. Our faith no longer lies in ourselves but in Christ. We no longer belong to ourselves but to Him. We learn to love the law just as God loves us.

Now that I have learned these truths, I know the deep joy that comes from living in my true identity. I no longer experience fleeting moments of warmth and love as I did as a child. Now, I bathe in warmth and rejoice in His infinite love knowing that "I can do all things through Christ."[304]

---

[302] Alma 30:44, The Book of Mormon.
[303] Matthew 18:3-4, Holy Bible, KJV.
[304] Philippians 4:13, Holy Bible, KJV.

God needs YOU and the unique gifts that only you can offer. Don't allow feelings of inadequacy to keep you from sharing yourself. We are all His hands.

– Jodi L. Nicholes –

———8———
Becky Squire
Cultivating True Confidence

What will this day be like? I wonder.
What will my future be? I wonder.
I've always longed for adventure,
To do the things I've never dared.
Now here I'm facing adventure
Then why am I so scared?[305]

---

[305] The Sound of Music, lyrics retrieved from
https://www.stlyrics.com/lyrics/thesoundofmusic/ihaveconfidence.htm

I grew up listening to Maria von Trapp sing these words in the beloved musical, *The Sound of Music*. All she wanted to do with her life was to become a nun and serve God. That sounds pretty noble, right? But instead she was sent to be a governess in the home of a widowed naval captain with seven children. Do you think she doubted herself? Do you think she doubted God? In hindsight (and because I've watched the movie too many times to count) I can tell you that God was calling her on a more important adventure than the one she'd planned for herself.

We all face adventure. That might look like changing the life of a hostile naval captain and his seven mischievous children, or it could look like stepping out of your comfort zone to minister to a stranger in need. No matter what our adventure may be, I'm sure we can all relate to Maria. Thoughts of wonder and hope, doubt and fear. What's the matter with me? Does any of this sound familiar?

The scriptures tell us that we all have weaknesses but that there is a place for weakness in our spiritual progress: "And if men come unto me I will show unto them their weakness. I give unto men weakness that they may be humble; and my grace is sufficient for all men that humble themselves before me; for if they humble themselves before me, and have faith in me, then will I make weak things become strong unto them."[306]

It's easy to wallow in our own weaknesses. And if we do this, we will find that, consequently, we do not allow "weak things"[307] to "become strong."[308] Some of us allow this to occur in the name of humility. But, in reality, it's simply a lack of confidence.

What is confidence?

---

[306] Ether 12:27, The Book of Mormon.
[307] Ibid.
[308] Ibid.

I admit that years ago I would imagine a confident person as someone who stood out in a crowd: the popular girl in high school, or the loud and talkative mom in the neighborhood. I'm not saying these women *aren't* confident, but that the qualities of popularity or talkativeness don't *define* confidence.

What exactly is confidence? Confidence comes from a genuine love of others and yourself. Confidence doesn't need to be seen. It emanates naturally when we aren't preoccupied with our own weaknesses and appreciate our divine potential. Elder Glenn L. Pace said, "Ironically, both pride and a lack of self-confidence cause us to focus excessively on ourselves and to deny the power of God in our lives."[309]

The world might make you believe that confidence is all about how others view you. But true confidence isn't about you. It's about others.

In fact, the scriptures teach us how we can each gain confidence.

> *Let thy bowels also be full of charity towards all men, and to the household of faith, and let virtue garnish thy thoughts unceasingly; then shall thy confidence wax strong in the presence of God; and the doctrine of the priesthood shall distil upon thy soul as the dews from heaven.*[310]

The Lord endows us with confidence as we practice "charity towards all men." Think of the well-known saying *you get what you give*. There is truth found in those words and they can be applied to almost anything. Insecurity feeds insecurity. Happiness feeds happiness. Help others feel confident, and it will build *your* confidence in

---

[309] Pace, Glenn L. "Confidence in the Lord," General Conference April 1985

return. One way we can practice charity is to be generous in our offering of well-earned praise of others, thus helping them gain confidence as well.

Confidence isn't something you either have or don't have. Every one of us can build and grow confidence. In fact, you have unlimited potential and abilities that can strengthen your confidence every day. I'd like to share four ways we can build confidence as disciples of Jesus Christ.

Be Obedient

It sounds so simple, right? We are taught from our earliest years to obey our mother and father and to keep the commandments. The law of obedience is drilled into our minds, but do we really understand it, and how it gives us confidence?

The Savior's standard is clear and simple: "If ye love me, keep my commandments."[311] We must acknowledge that we can't love God without also loving His commandments. There is no gray area, there is only right and wrong. For example, a group of your friends start gossiping about another friend behind their back. When faced with this situation, it might seem like you have a few options. You could tell your friends to stop gossiping and stick up for the other friend. You could join in and tell them another juicy story. Or you could decide to not participate in gossip and just stay silent. In reality, there are only two options. Right and wrong. Staying silent is an example of what some perceive as a gray area. Choosing something bad over something worse is still choosing wrong. And on the flip side, when we faithfully observe some commandments, it doesn't

---

[310] Doctrine and Covenants 121:45.
[311] John 14:15, Holy Bible, KJV.

justify neglecting others. Selective obedience brings selective blessings and a lack of confidence.

As we practice obedience, we must also make sure we are doing these right things for the right reasons. The Lord knows our every thought and the intents of our heart. He knows why you offered to take dinner to your neighbor—whether you hoped others would notice and think highly of you, or whether you sincerely wanted to help a friend in need. He knows why you go to church—whether to socialize and check it off your to-do list, or whether you hope to become truly closer to Him.

"Your religion is not just about showing up for church on Sunday," President Nelson said at BYU's commencement exercises in 2014. "It is about showing up as a true disciple from Sunday morning through Saturday night—24/7. There is no such thing as a part-time disciple of the Lord Jesus Christ." Is the restored gospel a part of your life, or is it your whole life? True confidence increases when you are striving to live a consecrated life for the right reasons.

Of course, we aren't perfect, and we aren't expected to be. But there's a difference between trying your best and being casual in keeping the commandments. Do you actively try your best to keep the commandments? Or do you simply try your best to not break them? That's the difference between careful and casual. Sister Becky Craven explains, "there is a careful way and a casual way to do everything, including living the gospel. As we consider our commitment to the Savior, are we careful or casual?"[312]

It all comes down to your decisions. Every time we hear counsel from our leaders, we have a choice to make. We can either obey with exactness, or we can rationalize, thinking to ourselves "Well, that's great for those with addictions or who are just learning about the gospel, but it doesn't apply to me." Sister Craven continues, "we can rationalize all we want, but the fact is, there is not a right way to do the wrong thing!"[313]

> *"Confidence comes from a genuine love of others and yourself."*
>
> *- Becky Squire*

Obedience is ultimately revealed by our desire to draw closer to God. As I have walked through life, my main goal has always been to develop my relationship with Heavenly Father. I've prayed to know how to strengthen this relationship, and now I also pray for my children to build their relationship with Him. But recently, my perspective has started to change. Perhaps I've been praying for the wrong thing. Instead of trying to establish a better relationship with Heavenly Father, maybe I need to focus on my own obedience. Heavenly Father has already set the terms for our relationship. All He asks of us is to obey willingly.

Our relationship with God is already established in that *He* loves *us* with an everlasting love. Elder Neal A. Maxwell said, "It is *our* love for *Him* that remains to be developed... We must draw closer to God. But we are to worship, to adore, and to obey God, not build a better relationship with Him!"[314] Each of us can gain a sense of inner confidence and peace when we obey gospel principles.

Keep the Commandments

---

[312] Craven, Becky L. "Careful Versus Casual," General Conference April 2019
[313] Ibid.
[314] Ibid.

Several years ago, my husband was looking for a new job. Some recruiters asked him to apply for a position at a bank in Alaska. It sounded pretty exciting, especially since we had lived in Utah all of our lives and had recently been itching to move out of state. His first interview was online, and it went really well. As he learned more details about the job, it became even more enticing.

Throughout the entire process, my husband and I prayed for clear direction on whether to pursue the job. We never received an answer either way, so we decided to proceed. Finally, they asked him to travel to Alaska for an in-person interview. I decided to tag along and make a little trip out of it. We arrived the day before his interview and wanted to do some sight-seeing. We instantly fell in love with the city and agreed that it would be a dream to live there.

That evening we decided to grab a quick bite before crashing at the hotel. As we were waiting for our food to arrive, we were both lost deep in our own thoughts. Suddenly, at the exact same moment, we looked at each other with wide eyes. He asked me what my look was all about. I told him I just heard the words, "You can't move here." He confirmed that he had just heard those exact words also.

We were a little crushed. Everything about the job and the location were exactly what we wanted. But we could not deny our experience. So, my husband turned down the job offer. We had both been taught to listen to the Spirit and obey, and we both exercised a true desire to do just that. My husband found another great job and we have seen many blessings from our decision. As we obey the commandments, we have the evidence of blessings, feelings of accomplishment, and the confidence that everything will work out for our good.

Each of us has an important role to fill in building His kingdom on earth. The way to do this is clear: The Lord simply asks us to keep His commandments. If we are diligent in studying the scriptures and setting aside time for personal prayer, we will receive inspiration, and personal revelation. Then, it is through obedience that we can take that knowledge and put it into action. And each day we can come closer to God as we follow promptings to serve others, love one another, and obey.

Be Faithful

I recently asked my four children (ages eight to fifteen) to name the first principle of the gospel. Without much hesitation, they all answered, *faith*. You might agree with them, but it was actually a trick question. According to the Fourth Article of Faith[315], the first principle of the gospel is faith *in the Lord Jesus Christ*. And faith in the Lord Jesus Christ is another way we develop true confidence in our lives.

The Bible Dictionary says:

> ...*To have faith is to have confidence in something or someone. The Lord has revealed Himself and His perfect character, possessing in their fullness all the attributes of love, knowledge, justice, mercy, unchangeableness, power, and every other needful thing, so as to enable the mind of man to place confidence in Him without reservation.*[316]

---

[315] *The Articles of Faith*, Retrieved from www.comeuntochrist.org/articles/articles-of-faith
[316] *Faith. Definition of Faith in Bible Dictionary, Bible.* The Church of Jesus Christ of Latter-day Saints version.

Faith in Jesus Christ takes us beyond mere acceptance of the Savior's identity and existence. It requires complete confidence in His infinite and eternal redemptive power.

We wouldn't have The Church of Jesus Christ of Latter-day Saints without the faith and confidence of a young boy. The Restoration of the Gospel occurred as the result of great faith on the part of the Prophet Joseph Smith while he was in his early teens. The coming forth of the Book of Mormon was an act of faith in Jesus Christ on the part of ancient American prophets who wrote their revelations and spiritual experiences upon metal plates. They had faith that their record would be a significant part of a glorious restoration of the Gospel in latter days. The angel Moroni appeared to Joseph Smith on a September night in 1823 when he approached the Lord in faith. He later wrote, "For I had full confidence in obtaining a divine manifestation, as I previously had one."[317]

Each one of us can demonstrate the powerful faith that Joseph Smith exemplified. It's not always easy, but when we do, we build confidence.

President Hinckley said: "When I discuss faith, I do not mean it in an abstract sense. I mean it as a living, vital force with recognition of God as our Father and Jesus Christ as our Savior."[318] I believe that as we try our best to apply this statement in our life, our faith and our desire to be obedient will be strengthened.

The word *faith* is often used interchangeably with *belief* and *hope,* and it may be difficult to distinguish between these words. There is a

---

[317] Joseph Smith-History 1:29.
[318] Gordon B. Hinckley, "With All Thy Getting Get Understanding," *Ensign*, August 1988, p.5.

difference, however. Although we cannot have faith without belief and hope, we can believe without having faith.

If you have a hard time exercising faith in any aspect of the gospel, take a step back and focus on what you believe. If you're not sure what you believe, step back again and focus on hope. What do you hope to believe? Faith in Jesus Christ, in His words, in His Atonement, in His Church, in His prophets, is the foundation of spiritual hope. When there seems to be nothing else, there is always hope.

One important differentiating quality of faith is that it requires action. That's why it's not an abstract idea. But action is hindered by fear and doubt, therefore, doubt and fear diminish as one's faith increases. This may be unprecedented, but I don't think it's a coincidence that I'm writing this section on faith at this specific moment in my life. Let me give you a peek into the past – as you're reading this, but my present – as I'm writing.

Not even one week ago, the world was essentially shut down. COVID-19 (Corona Virus) is now a worldwide pandemic and affects billions every day. Only two days ago, amid all of this uncertainty, my home state of Utah experienced the largest earthquake recorded in the last 29 years. It has been a week for the history books. Indeed, the world is engulfed in doubt and fear. This doubt and fear is all over the news, social media, and is readily apparent in the voices of young and old. As a result, I have seriously re-evaluated how strong my faith really is.

As members of the Church of Jesus Christ of Latter-day Saints, we are blessed with the restored gospel of Jesus Christ *in our day*. This knowledge lifts us when we feel discouraged or troubled. We can be reassured that our efforts will bear fruit in the Lord's own due time, if we press forward through the trials of this life and the testing of our faith.

When grief hits, when tragedies overtake us, and when life hurts so much that we can't breathe, we can have faith that Christ will join with us in the yoke and pull in order to lighten our burdens. When we feel uncertain, alone, frustrated, angry, let down, disappointed, or estranged from God and His

> *"Obedience is ultimately revealed by our desire to draw closer to God."*
>
> - *Becky Squire*

restored Church, it may take an extra measure of effort and faith to become closer to Him. Ultimately, everything God invites and commands us to do is an expression of His love for us and His desire to give us the blessings reserved for the faithful. God has promised that all who live according to the covenants they have made with Him will, in His time, receive all His promised blessings.

Our Savior knows our circumstances. If we meet each of life's challenges with humility and faith, our Savior Jesus Christ can help us overcome doubt and fear.

Help Gather Israel

One of my earliest memories is a simple exercise my father taught me to build confidence. When I was approximately four years old, my dad was the bishop in our ward. I was a shy little girl and didn't particularly like it when adults would talk to me. I would often furrow my brow and turn away from them. One day, my dad knelt beside me and looked me straight in the eyes. "*You* are the bishop's daughter," he said. "People are watching you. I don't expect you to talk to everyone you see, but can you at least give them a smile?" From that moment on, I committed to smile at everyone I saw. Throughout my father's life, he has served in many church leadership roles including bishop and in two stake presidencies. He naturally emulates confidence and genuine love toward others. Recently, I was thanking him for this simple lesson he taught me many years ago. To my surprise, he said that confidence didn't come naturally to him. In fact, smiling at others was something he had to consciously tell himself to do every day.

"By small and simple things are great things brought to pass."[319]

My father's words still echo in my mind, but with a simple edit: "*You* are a member of The Church of Jesus Christ of Latter-day Saints. People are watching you."

As members of The Church of Jesus Christ of Latter-day Saints, we have great responsibility. We know the truth of the Restored Gospel and we need to share that truth with others. As we do so, we are participating in God's most important work.

President Nelson said, "the gathering of Israel is the most important thing taking place on Earth today. Nothing else compares in magnitude, in importance, in majesty. And if you choose to, you can be a part of it."[320]

We are gathering Israel when we share that truth, when we defend it, and when we live it. How are you sharing the truth? I've been aware of the urgency to spread the gospel throughout the world since I was

---

[319] Alma 37:6, The Book of Mormon.
[320] Nelson, Russell M. "Hope of Israel." *Worldwide Youth Devotional*, Church of Jesus Christ of Latter-day Saints, 3 June 2018,

a young girl. I dreamt of going on a mission and converting many. When I was 19 years old, I met my wonderful husband and got married. I wasn't able to serve a mission and worried that I had missed my chance to do God's important work. Obviously, there are other ways to be a missionary, but I admit that I mostly pictured myself knocking on my neighbor's door (who I didn't know very well) with a plate of cookies and inviting them to church. And that terrified me.

Luckily, missing out on missionary opportunities is not the case. Heavenly Father has asked that each of us use our spiritual gifts to share the light. If you have a natural ability to talk to anyone and befriend strangers, then maybe knocking on your neighbor's door to invite them to church will work for you. One of my favorite ways to share the light of Christ is to write. Back in 2007, I started a family blog (with almost everyone else). A few months later I heard Elder M. Russell Ballard suggest that we use the internet to be ambassadors of the gospel when he said, "may I ask that you join the conversation by participating on the Internet to share the gospel and to explain in simple and clear terms the message of the Restoration."[321] Using my blog to share the gospel? Brilliant!

Sharing the gospel takes confidence, but I believe it will happen naturally when we use our own, unique spiritual gifts. Do you know what your spiritual gifts are?

The scriptures list several spiritual gifts such as the gift of wisdom, knowledge, faith, healing, miracles, prophecy, discerning, and the gift of tongues. They also include the gift of a testimony of Christ and the ability to believe the testimonies of others.[322] Other spiritual

www.churchofjesuschrist.org/study/broadcasts/worldwide-devotional-for-young-adults/2018/06/hope-of-israel?lang=eng.
[321] Ballard, M. Russell. "Sharing the Gospel Using the Internet," *Ensign*, July 2008, p.63.
[322] Doctrine and Covenants 46:7-29.

gifts not listed specifically in the scriptures, but nevertheless implied, may include the gifts of listening, humor, joy, humility, charity, love, hope, and confidence.

Have you ever prayed for a specific spiritual gift? We are encouraged to "seek ye earnestly the best gifts, always remembering for what they are given."[323] In the scriptures, we read of many people with spiritual gifts. Adam's gift of prophecy, Enoch's faith which allowed him to perform miracles, Abraham's unwavering exact obedience, Sarah's patience, Ruth's loyalty, Peter's gift of healing, the brother of Jared's gift of asking, Alma the younger's humility, and Moroni's testimony. All of these are gifts of the spirit. Do you think these individuals were born with these qualities, or do you think perhaps they prayed for them?

Throughout all my adult life, I have had a desire to learn all I can about the scriptures and principles of the gospel. This desire started out like a small flame, warm yet barely noticeable. After reading my patriarchal blessing several years ago, I felt prompted to put more thought into gaining more knowledge. And every time I put the work in, that small flame of desire to learn grew and grew. One day, a member of my bishopric met with me to extend a new calling: Gospel Doctrine teacher. Those words terrified me, but I accepted.

Three years later, I'm still terrified every time I walk into the classroom to begin teaching, but I can testify that this experience has helped me learn much about the scriptures and the gospel, much more than I ever could have done on my own. I had a desire for the gift of knowledge, and Heavenly Father blesses me as I pray and prepare. If our intentions are pure, I know we will be blessed with the spiritual gifts we desire.

---

[323] Ibid.

Sheri L. Dew reminds us of other spiritual gifts we have as women of the gospel: "Noble and great. Courageous and determined. Faithful and fearless. That is who you are, and who you have always been. And understanding it can change your life, because this knowledge carries a confidence that cannot be duplicated any other way."[324]

True confidence is understanding your power to influence. *Influence* is somewhat of a buzzword right now, isn't it? It has more meaning than it did ten years ago. The online world is full of *influencers*. But real influence doesn't come from followers or numbers.

Sister Neill F. Marriott said, "Our small acts of faith and service are how most of us can continue in God and eventually bring eternal light and glory to our family, our friends, and our associates. You truly carry a circle of influence with you!"[325]

We need more women who constantly share goodness, even if only one person hears it. Think about your circle of influence. Your influence will have a ripple effect. It starts with you. You immediately influence those individuals you interact with every day, perhaps your husband, children, co-workers, siblings, and so on. Your husband influences his co-workers. Your kids influence their friends. Your co-workers influence their families. And it goes on and on and on.

Now the question you must ask yourself is what are you going to do to be the kind of influence you want to be? Will you invite your neighbors over? Will you go to the temple more often? Will you study your scriptures every day? M. Russell Ballard wrote, "We

---

[324] Dew, Sheri L. "Knowing Who You Are-and Who You Have Always Been." *The Church Historian's Press*, 19 Apr. 2016, www.churchhistorianspress.org/at-the-pulpit/part-4/Chapter-48?lang=eng.
[325] Marriott, Neill F. "Sharing Your Light," General Conference October 2014

need more of the distinctive, influential voices and faith of women. We need them to learn the doctrine and to understand what we believe so that they can bear their testimonies about the truth of all things."[326] When we follow the example of Jesus Christ, the greatest influencer of all, we will have the confidence to be the kind of women Elder Ballard described.

> "We need more women who constantly share goodness, even if only one person hears it."
>
> - Becky Squire

If you feel discouraged, pray to know how you can be an influence. You are a daughter of God with work to do. I echo Harriet Uchtdorf's words when she wrote, "You ... are vibrant and enthusiastic beacons in an ever-darkening world as you show, through the way you live your lives, that the gospel is a joyful message."[327]

Every one of us has an important part in the gathering of Israel. "It is not possible to truly love yourself unless you love what is truly you, and that is the whole house of Israel in which you belong."[328] We must use our unique spiritual gifts to be a positive influence in the gathering of Israel, and being able to do that starts with confidence.

Keep Covenants

---

[326] Ballard, M. Russell. "Men and Women and Priesthood Power," *Ensign*, September, 2014, p.28.

[327] Uchtdorf, Harriet R. *The Light We Share*, Deseret Book Company, Salt Lake City, 2014, p.41.

[328] Madsen, Truman G. "Elijah's Mission." *BYU Speeches*, 5 May 1977, speeches.byu.edu/talks/truman-g-madsen/elijahs-mission/.

Confidence comes through understanding and keeping our covenants. Sheri Dew states, "I believe that the moment we learn to unleash the full influence of converted, covenant-keeping women, the kingdom of God will change overnight."[329]

Covenant keeping is ever more crucial with each passing day. As the world becomes more and more wicked, we need women who become more and more steadfast. Joseph Smith in Joseph-Smith Matthew 1:22 indicates that in the last days even the "very elect … according to the covenant" will be deceived. Each and every sister, young woman, and child who has been baptized has made covenants with Heavenly Father, both the struggling and the strong, the questioning and the converted, and the afflicted and the comforted. All are at risk of being deceived by false teachings. Sister Bonnie L. Oscarson counseled, "To be converted covenant keepers, we need to study the essential doctrines of the gospel and have an unshakable testimony of their truthfulness."[330]

Sister Oscarson's words echo Elder Ballard's. *Study doctrine and then share your testimony of its truth.* Do you feel the urgency behind this principle? When we study and know true doctrine, we can share it with more confidence.

Do you have confidence in the doctrines of the gospel? Think about how you feel when talking about the doctrines of the gospel with those who are not Latter-day Saints. Many of us anticipate criticism and expect the need to defend ourselves. But again, that's all about how others view you. It's not true confidence. When we have confidence in gospel principles, we will have confidence in our testimony.

---

[329] Dew, Sheri L. "Stand Tall and Stand Together," General Conference October 2000
[330] Oscarson, Bonnie L. "Rise Up in Strength Sisters in Zion," General Conference October 2016

A good idea is to regularly evaluate your personal beliefs. Do you have confidence in your testimony of Jesus Christ? Is it truly a sustaining power in your life, or is it more of a hope that what you have learned is true? Hope is an essential step, but it won't do much good when you inevitably face the serious challenges of life. Does your testimony guide you to choose the right? Your testimony can and should be an essential part of who you are. If an honest evaluation of your testimony leaves you feeling that it's not where you want it to be, today is the day to get to work.

Moroni taught, "Faith is things which are hoped for and not seen; wherefore, dispute not because ye see not, for ye receive no witness until after the trial of your faith."[331] That means you must take action! As you live the principles of the gospel consistently, your testimony will grow, and your confidence will strengthen. Faith produces a steady stream of tender mercies and even mighty miracles that go hand in hand with spiritual confidence. And they will reveal themselves more as you strive to choose the right.

Sister Oscarson also warned, "If we don't teach our children and youth true doctrine—and teach it clearly—the world will teach them Satan's lies."[332] I think that we should apply this same counsel to ourselves. If we don't search and study true doctrine, the world will deceive us with Satan's lies. Some of the most common lies are that Heavenly Father is disappointed in you, that you are unworthy, that the Atonement of Jesus Christ is beyond your reach, that there is no point in even trying, that everyone else is better than you, and a million other variations.

Not only is living the gospel this way unhealthy, it's completely unnecessary! The decision to change is yours, and yours alone.

---

[331] Ether 12:6, The Book of Mormon.
[332] Oscarson, Bonnie L. "Rise Up in Strength Sisters in Zion," General Conference October 2016

Spiritual confidence increases when you take responsibility for your own spiritual well-being by applying the Atonement of Jesus Christ daily.

I used to avoid the topic of confidence because it can carry a connotation of being puffed up and prideful. However, when I changed my way of thinking, I realized true confidence comes when I'm striving to become closer to God and when I keep His commandments. Confidence is something I work on every day. Some days it manifests itself easily; some days I have to work harder than ever, but I know that through Jesus Christ I can do all things.[333]

You Can Find Your Confidence

Remember that true confidence is not about you – it's about others. And as you take these steps to: 1) increase your obedience; 2) exercise faith in Jesus Christ; 3) help gather Israel; and 4) keep your covenants; you will have true confidence – confidence in the Savior, Jesus Christ, and confidence in yourself.

You have and will continue to face trials throughout your life. You'll experience doubt and fear. It's all part of the adventure of life. After all, it wouldn't be an adventure without the ups and downs! As a former nun, Maria von Trapp relied on her faith to find true confidence, which came through Jesus Christ. Let us all remember how Maria finished that hopeless beginning of her beautiful song:

> *All I trust I leave my heart to,*
> *All I trust becomes my own!*

---

[333] Philippians 4:13, Holy Bible, KJV.

I have confidence in confidence alone!
Besides, which you see, I have confidence in me![334]

---

[334] The Sound of Music, lyrics retrieved from
https://www.stlyrics.com/lyrics/thesoundofmusic/ihaveconfidence.htm

Spiritual confidence increases when you take responsibility for your own spiritual well-being by applying the Atonement of Jesus Christ daily.

— Becky Squire —

—9—
Tiffany Fletcher

Your House of Light

The Key to Overcoming Darkness is Light

When I was a child, I faced many dark days struggling to feel God's light due to my mother's mental illness. She suffered from Dissociative Identity Disorder and had 14 different alters, including a violent male alter named Bill. With my mom's "multiple personalities," every day was different and many days were frightening.

Because of the darkness that shrouded my childhood, I've sought after light my entire life. This search has given me a tremendous admiration for lighthouses because of their strength and beauty. A lighthouse is what I want to be.

But lighthouses are more than just a beacon to me—they are a house of light, much like the temple. These houses of light serve as beacons to the world and help bring people out of darkness.

Because of the dark and difficult days of my childhood, I've always wanted to create a house of light—a lighthouse—for my own family. I want my children to feel that our home is a refuge from the storm and a place of safety and peace.

Line upon line, as we've strived to fortify our home with study and prayer, testimony and faith, covenant and sacrifice, we've discovered that God's light is essential to all we do. His light is the driving force in all that is good, all that is holy, and all that is precious in our life. We aren't perfect, by any stretch of the imagination, but line upon line we continue to build our house. And step by step, we're coming closer to Christ.

In these days of darkness and sorrow, of trial and tribulation, it is essential that we all learn how to build our own house of light. The best way to build a lighthouse is to build it in the same manner as God's house of light.

In the Doctrine and Covenants, when the Lord commanded the Saints to build a temple He said: "Organize yourselves; prepare every needful thing; and establish a house, even a house of prayer, a house of fasting, a house of faith, a house of learning, a house of glory, a house of order, a house of God."[335]

A house of light is built line upon line, just like God's temple. I've learned that the order is important, and prayer is the foundation. If we learn how to pray with power, we'll have God's Spirit to be with us. He will teach us every single thing we need to know in order to create our own house of light and withstand the current darkness of this world and all that may lay ahead.

---

[335] Doctrine and Covenants 88:119.

Our outcome in the battle with darkness is dependent on our willingness to pray with real intent and our obedience to the personal revelation we receive as a result of those prayers.

Light Versus Darkness

One of the greatest examples of prayer the world has ever known is the humble prayer of Joseph Smith while he was in the sacred grove. Throughout history, we have many recorded events where the Lord spoke to God's children. But there are very few recorded events where God Himself came down in person to speak to man on earth.

This was one of the greatest events in all of human history. And certainly, the greatest event in this dispensation. But just prior to that beautiful and sacred experience where God the Father and Jesus Christ appeared to Joseph Smith, there was another event that happened in that very same sacred grove.

This event is vital to our understanding of that incredible experience, but it's rarely discussed and often discarded. In his own words, when describing his attempt to pray, Joseph recounted the following:

> *I had scarcely done so, when immediately I was seized upon by some power which entirely overcame me, and had such an astonishing influence over me as to bind my tongue so that I could not speak.*[336]

Joseph continued to say that thick darkness gathered around him and he felt doomed to destruction. Satan knew what was about to happen in that sacred grove. He understood the overwhelming light that would cover the earth from that singular prayer, and he exerted all his efforts to try and stop it. But Joseph resisted, calling on God to rescue him, and only then did the glorious First Vision come.

There's an important lesson that we can learn from Joseph's experience with the forces of darkness. That lesson is this: Satan is real. He will come before each of us many times in our life to try and stop us from completing the work God has sent us here to do. This was true for Joseph's time and it is equally true for you and me today.

---

[336] Joseph Smith History 1:15, The Pearl of Great Price.

The battle that we fought in the pre-existence is the same battle we fight in our mortal life. Only the enemy is more difficult to see, and it will require more than our natural eyes to recognize his influence.

If we want to overcome the adversarial darkness that is sure to invade our lives, we must do all we can to understand our enemy.

The Final Battle Ground

Satan has been at this game for millennia. He knows us, and he knows our weaknesses. He also knows that because we love God, we will not willingly sin against Him. But Satan is clever. Instead of trying to get us to sin in the big things, he seeks to influence us in small and subtle ways by attacking our minds and hearts.

We've been taught all our lives that God's Spirit speaks to our minds and hearts, and Satan knows this. Satan knows that if he can fill our minds with doubt, or fear, or pride, or lust, or any other unholy thought, that he can block us from receiving personal revelation from our Heavenly Father.

Satan knows that personal revelation is essential to get us through these last days. So, he shrouds our mind in darkness and seeks to harden our hearts so that we are past feeling and lose our ability to communicate with the still small whisperings of the Spirit.

> "*The key to developing a sound mind lies in our ability to clear out the darkness that surrounds us and to increase our light by focusing our hearts and minds on the Savior.*"
>
> *- Tiffany Fletcher*

Satan plagues women with depression and doubts about their self-worth. He tells them they're never *enough* and strips them of their courage to speak. He plagues men with pornography and self-loathing, and overwhelms them with guilt and shame. He reminds them of their weaknesses and strips them of their courage to fight so that they give in to those weaknesses.

Satan fills our hearts with anger and hatred, pride and arrogance, sadness and sorrow. He does all this to keep the focus of our minds from the things of God, so that rather than centering our thoughts and hearts on the Savior, we're just trying to survive the darkness.

We are absolutely fighting the same war we were fighting in heaven. But today, the battlefield is primarily our mind.

For some, this may bring a sense of fear. But, as Paul said in Timothy, "For God hath not given us the spirit of fear; but of power and of love, and of a sound mind."[337] The Lord gave very similar counsel to Joseph Smith and the early Saints: "Look to me in every thought; doubt not, fear not."[338] The Lord knew that Satan would use doubt and fear to stop us from progressing. Because of this, the first words from many of the heavenly messengers who've visited the earth were these: "Fear Not!"

Fear can stop us in our tracks and keep us from moving forward in God's plan of progression. With the Lord's help, we can fight this battle, overcome doubt and fear, and ultimately win the war—just like so many warriors before us.

The Victory of a Sound Mind

Captain Moroni in the Book of Mormon was one of the greatest warriors this world has ever known. As a matter of fact, this is what's written about him:

> *If all men had been, and were, and ever would be, like unto Moroni, behold, the very powers of hell would have been shaken forever; yea, the devil would never have power over the hearts of the children of men.*[339]

Why was this said about Captain Moroni? It's because, while every other military leader in history has focused their fighting on the physical and temporal aspects of war, Captain Moroni had a different approach. Before he ever began throwing up towers and digging trenches, brandishing weapons and armoring soldiers,

---

[337] 2 Timothy 1:7, Holy Bible, KJV.
[338] Doctrine and Covenants 6:36.
[339] Alma 48:17, The Book of Mormon.

Moroni, unlike other military leaders, "had been preparing the minds of the people to be faithful unto the Lord their God."[340]

Moroni knew that if the minds of his people were strong, they would have the power to fight their enemy and to overcome. This is because Moroni knew who his enemy was. The enemy wasn't the Lamanites. The enemy was the adversary and the doubts and fears he would surely use to conquer Moroni's army before the physical battle was ever waged.

Moroni knew that a sound mind focused on the Savior was a sure victory for all of them. And Moroni wasn't the only Book of Mormon military leader who knew this. In describing the two-thousand stripling warriors, Helaman said, "Now this was the faith of these of whom I have spoken; they are young, and their minds are firm, and they do put their trust in God continually."[341] A sound mind was the weapon of every mighty Book of Mormon warrior who ever faced the enemy and won.

Imagine what would happen if every person today was like Captain Moroni. Satan would be bound and the millennium would begin. President Spencer W. Kimball said, "When Satan is bound in a single home—when Satan is bound in a single life—the Millennium has already begun in that home, in that life."[342]

We are in the most difficult battle we have ever faced. But victory can and will be ours. If we can learn to conquer our thoughts, Satan will be bound in our lives. We will know the will of God for us, and together, we will usher in the second coming of our Savior.

The Miracles of Jesus

The key to developing a sound mind lies in our ability to clear out the darkness that surrounds us and to increase our light by focusing our hearts and minds on the Savior.

Satan spends every hour of every day striving to get men's hearts to fail them. We are even told that in the last days, emotional and

---

[340] Alma 48:7, The Book of Mormon.
[341] Alma 57:27, The Book of Mormon.
[342] Kimball, Edward L. *The Teachings of Spencer W. Kimball*. Deseret Book Company, Salt Lake City, 1982, p.172.

psychological struggles are a sign of the times. Satan goes about seeking whom he can devour. He uses well-honed tactics to convince us that the lies he tells us are true. He can speak partial truths. He can even transform himself into an angel of light.

Satan is constantly whispering in our ears, just like he did to Adam and Eve in the Garden of Eden. He's reminding us of our weaknesses, encouraging us to act on our lusts, deceiving us with all kinds of falsehoods that closely masquerade as the truth, and presenting us with all manner of temptation.

> *"We are those who believe."*
>
> *- Tiffany Fletcher*

How, then, can we overcome Satan's powerful tactics if Satan is bent on destroying us and spends his days wreaking havoc and creating chaos in the minds and hearts of God's children? How can we not be deceived by the craftiness and subtleness of the devil? The answer is simple, yet seldom discussed. We do just as Jesus did—we cast Satan out.

It's interesting to me that in nearly every city Jesus traveled to, the scriptures say that Jesus cast out devils and healed the sick. Yet in our world today, we give blessings to heal the sick and talk about the power of healing through our faith. But we rarely, if ever, talk about casting out devils.

Mark, in the New Testament, recorded: "And he healed many that were sick of diverse diseases, and cast out many devils."[343] Also speaking of Jesus, Matthew wrote, "When the even was come, they brought unto him many that were possessed with devils: and he cast out the spirits with his word, and healed all that were sick."[344] Even when King Benjamin was telling his people of the Savior and what He would do when He came, he repeated the words of the angel who spoke to him and said, "And he shall cast out devils, or the evil spirits which dwell in the hearts of the children of men."[345]

---

[343] Mark 1:34, Holy Bible, KJV.
[344] Matthew 8:16, Holy Bible, KJV.
[345] Mosiah 3:6, The Book of Mormon.

Did you catch that? Evil spirits dwell in the hearts of men and Jesus casts them out. But who casts devils out today? As disciples of Jesus Christ, this is one of the miracles we've been given charge over. Devils are still among us, and are now in an even greater number than the time of Jesus, as darkness continues to descend. And devils aren't just with the sinners, they torment each of us. Just as the Savior cast seven devils out of Mary Magdalene, we must cast out the devils in our own lives.

If you're reading this and saying to yourself, "Well, of course Jesus cast out devils. He's the son of God. But who am I to cast out devils," let me share with you what the Lord told his twelve apostles: "And these signs shall follow them that believe; In my name shall they cast out devils."[346] Or, if you're justifying, "Well there are no devils in our day," let me share with you what the Lord said to Joseph Smith and the early Saints: "And these signs shall follow them that believe... in my name they shall do many wonderful works; In my name, they shall cast out devils; in my name they shall heal the sick."[347] The Lord also said these words: "Require not miracles, except I shall command you, except casting out devils [and] healing the sick."[348]

The Lord clearly wants us to cast out the devils that surround us— those that dwell in both our mind and heart. This is one of the few miracles we are allowed to do without an express commandment from Him telling us to do so. He knows the devil seeks to destroy us, and He's given us a powerful way to fight back.

The ability to cast out devils isn't just something a man holding the priesthood can do. As covenant-keeping women, we too have the power to cast out devils. Our access to the power of the priesthood is dependent on our faith and is evident in the covenants we make in the temple. The Lord told the early Saints, "And whoso shall ask it in my name in faith, they shall cast out devils; they shall heal the sick...cause the blind to receive their sight...the deaf to hear...the dumb to speak...and the lame to walk."[349]

---

[346] St. Mark 16:17, Holy Bible, KJV.
[347] Doctrine and Covenants 84:65-68.
[348] Doctrine and Covenants 24:13.
[349] Doctrine and Covenants 35:9.

We are those who believe. And through our faith and by calling upon the name of Jesus Christ, we can and will perform some of God's greatest miracles in these final days as we help to prepare the earth—and its people—for the second coming of our Savior.

In an address to the sisters of the Church, President Russell M. Nelson said: "We need women who know how to make important things happen by their faith."[350] This must surely include casting out devils.

The Lord's own words are evidence that He expects us to cast out devils and has given us the sufficient power to do so. Through the power of our faith, we can courageously and confidently exercise the power of the priesthood, say a prayer, and boldly cast Satan out of our lives.

The Purpose of Prayer

The prayer of faith is one of the greatest tools we have as women in our arsenal against the adversary. Boyd K. Packer stated, "There are few things more powerful than the faithful prayers of a righteous mother."[351] We are all mothers by virtue of who we are eternally. Therefore, this quote applies to each covenant woman. There are few things in this world that are more powerful than our faithful prayers. And our prayers are vital for these last days.

Some variation of "pray always," "pray continually," and "always pray," is repeated nearly fifty times in the scriptures. Nearly all of these accounts include the reason prayer is so important, "that you may overcome Satan at the last day." Here are some examples: "Pray always, that you may come off conqueror; yea, that you may conquer Satan, and that you may escape the hands of the servants of Satan that do uphold his work;"[352] "Verily, verily, I say unto you, ye must watch and pray always, lest ye be tempted by the devil, and ye be led away captive by him."[353] "Watch ye therefore, and pray always, that ye may be accounted worthy to escape all

---

[350] Nelson, Russell M. "A Plea to My Sisters." General Conference October 2015
[351] Packer, Boyd K. "These Things I Know." General Conference April 2013
[352] Doctrine and Covenants 10:5.
[353] 3 Nephi 18:15, The Book of Mormon.

these things that shall come to pass, and to stand before the Son of man."[354]

According to the law of witnesses, "In the mouth of two or three witnesses shall every word be established."[355] When warnings and phrases are repeated several times throughout the scriptures, we can know those lessons, principles, and precepts are important to the Lord. When the Lord's words are repeated by the mouths of the prophets throughout the scriptures, the message is essential to God's plan for us and we need to pay attention. This is done so that we can be certain of those things that we should do. It is given for our understanding and learning, and to teach us those things we need for salvation.

These guidelines and admonitions aren't just suggestions; they are vital to our safety and protection. Many different prophets warned of our day and entreated us to "pray always" in order to overcome the darkness. The Savior Himself added His own testimony to the importance of this sacred act. He said, "Verily, verily, I say unto you, ye must watch and pray always... Behold I am the light; I have set an example for you."[356]

> *"Prayer is also how we will fill our home with the Savior's powerful and healing light."*
>
> *- Tiffany Fletcher*

The Lord taught that He is our light. He also taught that by watching and praying always, we will have the power to resist temptation: "for Satan desireth to have you, that he may sift you as wheat. Therefore ye must always pray unto the Father in my name."[357] The Lord went on to teach that both individual and family prayers are

---

[354] St. Luke 21:36, Holy Bible, KJV.
[355] Doctrine and Covenants 6:28; Ether 5:4, The Book of Mormon; Matthew 18:16, Holy Bible, KJV.
[356] 3 Nephi 18:15-25, The Book of Mormon.
[357] Ibid.

essential: "Pray in your families unto the Father, always in my name, that your wives and your children may be blessed."[358]

In addition to the significance of the repetition of prayer in the Lord's sermon, there is another principle that is important for us to understand. Christ said: "Therefore, hold up your light that it may shine unto the world. Behold, I am the light which ye shall hold up—that which ye have seen me do."[359] How do we hold up this light? And what is it they had just witnessed the Savior do? "Behold ye see that I have prayed unto the Father, and ye all have witnessed... and whosoever breaketh this commandment suffereth himself to be led into temptation."[360]

They had just witnessed Christ praying to the Father. This insight helps us to recognize that prayer allows us to access the light that we have been asked to hold up. Prayer is also how we will fill our home with the Savior's powerful and healing light.

As we pray always, unto the Father in the name of Christ, our home will be allowed a greater portion of light that we may then hold up to the world. This light will be essential to us as we attempt to walk through darkness. We will not see through the fog without it. Prayer is absolutely vital to fulfilling our mission here on Earth and to help prepare the world for Christ's second coming. Prayer will give us access to the light that will fortify our minds, bring God's light into our homes, and help lead ourselves and others out of darkness.

One Final Thought

Elder Packer said: "For while virtue, by choice, will not associate with filth, evil cannot tolerate the presence of light."[361] Did you hear that? Evil cannot tolerate the presence of light! This means that the more we seek to make ourselves and our homes houses of light—or lighthouses—the more we cast out the darkness. I wish I had space in this book to share everything I've learned about overcoming

---

[358] Ibid.

[359] Ibid.

[360] Ibid.

[361] Packer, Boyd K. "Worthy Music, Worthy Thoughts." Adapted from an October 1973 General Conference Address, *New Era*, Apr. 2008, www.churchofjesuschrist.org/study/new-era/2008/04/worthy-music-worthy-thoughts?lang=eng.

darkness with light. But know this: with prayer as the foundation of your lighthouse, the Lord will tell you everything else you need to know.

I want to leave you with this quote. It was counsel given to Joseph Smith from the angel Moroni. This account was written by Orson Hyde and can be found in the Joseph Smith Papers.[362] According to Orson Hyde, Moroni showed Joseph the darkness that was around him so that he could know the good from the evil. He then said, "Now go your way and remember what the Lord has done for you. Be diligent in keeping his commandments and he will deliver you from the temptations, persecutions, and snares of the evil one."[363]

Moroni then finished his message by summing up everything I've shared with you and the same advice I am certain Moroni would give each of us if he were here: "Don't forget to pray that your mind may become strong, that you may have power to escape the evil when the Lord shall reveal himself unto you, so that you may receive these precious things."[364] Moroni told Joseph to pray for a strong mind so that he would have the power to escape the evil that comes, especially that which comes just before the Lord reveals Himself, like He did in the sacred grove. This is counsel we can all use in our day-to-day life, especially as we move closer to that glorious day when the Lord will reveal Himself to each of us.

But as a writer and editor, I value the meaning and beauty in punctuation. So, in tweaking this quote with a simple comma, my counsel is also this: "Don't forget to pray, that your mind may become strong, that you may have power to escape the evil when the Lord shall reveal himself unto you, so that you may receive these precious things."[365] There are so many precious things the Lord wants to reveal to us, but He can't until our minds are strong enough

---

[362] *The Joseph Smith Papers: A Comprehensive Digital Collection of the Papers of Joseph Smith*, Intellectual Reserve, Inc., Retrieved from www.josephsmithpapers.org/.

[363] Hyde, Orson. "Ein Ruf Aus Der Wüste (A Cry out of the Wilderness), 1842, Extract, English Translation." *The Joseph Smith Papers: A Comprehensive Digital Collection of the Papers of Joseph Smith*, Intellectual Reserve, Inc., Retrieved from www.josephsmithpapers.org/transcript/orson-hyde-ein-ruf-aus-der-wste-a-cry-out-of-the-wilderness-1842-extract-english-translation?print=true.

[364] Ibid.

[365] Ibid. punctuation added.

to resist the darkness that is sure to come before any increase of light.

Your faithful prayers, both individually and as a family, are vital to the strength of your home and the people within it. Those prayers will also strengthen your mind and allow you to overcome the darkness that's all around you—here in our day—just prior to the Lord revealing Himself in His glorious second coming. Prayer is the light, both in your home and in your heart, that will enable you to create a strong and beautiful house of light—a lighthouse of the Lord.

As we pray always,
unto the Father in
the name of Christ,
our home will be allowed
a greater portion of
light that we may then
hold up to the world.

– Tiffany Fletcher –

——10——
Rhonda Steed

Women Who Gather

The Bay of Fundy on the coast of Nova Scotia, Canada is one of the most beautiful places a person can visit. It is well known for having some of the highest tides in the world. Over 160 billion tons of water move in and out of the Bay of Fundy every day, twice a day. You can see a huge portion of the native red soil that covers the area and find shells and other treasures scattered all over the ocean floor if you are there at the right time of the day.

In 2017 we took our three oldest children to visit a beautiful provincial park that is part of the Bay of Fundy. When we first arrived at the park, the tide was out, which meant there were hundreds of feet of the red sand left that would be covered with the ocean in just a few hours' time.

We brought buckets and shovels to play in the sand and after running for a bit, my son Eli started building. He was eight at the time and loved to build in the sand. Eli would first start digging a big hole so that he could make a castle. There's a huge distance that fills with water every day and it moves back in relatively fast. Eli had started building right next to the water and about the time he had built one castle wall, the tide was filling his hole and making it impossible to build. He saw what was happening to his work. He stopped, gathered his tools and treasures, then moved ten steps away from the water and started to work again. Ten minutes later he was having the same problem.

Each time Eli was being overrun with water, he would stop his work, gather his tools and treasures, move and then start again. My husband and I watched him, marveling that he didn't get frustrated. He never even stopped to watch his previous castle beginnings getting flooded away. He just gathered his tools and treasures to keep moving them all out of the way of the water so that none of it would be lost. He never regretted the work he did, even though it was repeatedly undone. He was completely focused on his purpose that day and he kept working at it despite the ocean working against him.

Called to be a Gatherer

This experience made me think of the growing feeling among women in the Church of Jesus Christ of Latter-day Saints that God has a work for us to do. I hear it from the women I know and interact with. It can sound like "I feel like I'm supposed to do something but

196

I'm not sure where or what." It is a woman's longing to understand where God needs her and what she is to do.

In 1979 Spencer W. Kimball prophesied about the growth in the church in the last days: "Much of the major growth that is coming to the Church in the last days will come because many of the good women of the world [in whom there is often such an inner sense of spirituality] will be drawn to the Church in large numbers."[366]

President Kimball shared the things that will draw those righteous women in. First, that the women of the Church are righteous. We need to be righteous to be someone that other women can look to and learn from. Second, women of the church need to be articulate. Being articulate means that we can express our ideas and feelings fluently and coherently. The other meaning of articulate is to form a joint between two pieces. If you apply that meaning in this context it could mean that the women of the church help bridge the Gospel into other religious women's lives. If I build a relationship with one woman and she knows the church because of me, I am helping to join her to the women of the Church.

There is one other important thing President Kimball points out about this major growth that is going to happen. It will all depend on the women of the church being seen as "distinct and different—in happy ways" from the world. We have to be different from the world and we need to be happy about it.

Doesn't that just stir something inside you? It sure does for me.

This quote has been referenced multiple times in the years since it was given, most notably in 2015 when Russell M. Nelson (an apostle at the time) gave a talk in general conference called "A Plea to My Sisters." He was practically begging the women of the church to stand up and be seen. He said:

My dear sisters, you have special spiritual gifts and propensities. Tonight, I urge you, with all the hope of my heart, to pray to understand *your spiritual gifts*—to cultivate, use, and expand them, even more than you ever have.[367]

So many things stick out to me in this quote and make me feel fired up. A big one is the line he gives next. "You will change the world as you do so."[368]

The women of the church have been told by prophets of God that we can change the world. He taught us that we each have spiritual gifts that we can use to help God in His work to gather Israel. President Nelson went on to talk about how he and his wife invited all of the youth to enlist in what he called the Lord's youth battalion to help gather Israel on both sides of the veil. Both sides of the veil means the living and the dead. This work is the greatest challenge, cause and work on the earth. He went on to say:

It is a cause that desperately needs women, because women shape the future. So tonight, I'm extending a prophetic plea to you, the women of the Church, to shape the future by helping to gather scattered Israel.[369]

The women of the church are called to play a major role in the gathering of Israel in these latter days. The Lord has things for us to

---

[366] Kimball, Spencer W. "The Role of Righteous Women," General Conference October 1979
[367] Nelson, Russell M. "A Plea to My Sisters," General Conference October 2015
[368] Ibid.

do. Not only that, He is saying there are special things for each one of us to do with our individual spiritual gifts.

A prophet of God has asked each of us to expand, cultivate, and to use our own special spiritual gifts to help gather scattered Israel. He was very direct. That "growing feeling"[370] among the women—it is the same calling. We feel it inside us, even if we aren't sure what it looks like.

Expanding, cultivating and using our own special spiritual gifts.

Belle S. Spafford spoke about women helping the work along. She taught that women of the church can help women of the world with their training, their leadership skills and their testimonies. The church provides opportunities for women to lead large groups of other women, children and teenagers. Women in the Relief Society can be a big power for helping women all over the world bring change to the world. She said:

"Guided by Church teachings, they can help themselves to move forward along proper lines in the development of their talents and skills and in their service to mankind."[371]

Sister Spafford said that unfortunately some women in the church are unable to do this for the women of the world because they do not know the doctrine well enough to teach it. We need to know what the doctrine is and then have the courage to follow it no matter the world's opinion. We have to know it to use it.

---

[369] Ibid.
[370] Ibid.
[371] Spafford, Belle S. "Latter-day Saint Women in Today's Changing World." *BYU Speeches*, 11 Feb. 1979, speeches.byu.edu/talks/belle-s-spafford/latter-day-saint-women-todays-changing-world/

The cool thing about serving in the Church of Jesus Christ of Latter-day Saints is that God gives us opportunities to learn skills through our different roles we fill in the church.

For example, when you serve in a Primary presidency you learn skills of managing time, teaching, working with a budget, public speaking, helping teachers succeed, giving directions; all kinds of lessons that can be applied in other areas of life. The opportunities the church gives women (as well as men and children) gives them an avenue to learn many valuable skills.

If we know the doctrine of the gospel and learn the skills God intends us to, we will be able and prepared to do what God asks of us. We will be articulate and righteous. Then we will be a light that can draw women of the world to Jesus Christ and his church.

The world needs us, the women of the Church of Jesus Christ of Latter-day Saints. We need to stand beside them, helping in the ways only the women of the gospel can. The brethren have pleaded with us in the last few years to take our place at leading the women of the world to find Jesus Christ.

Satan knows the great power that is in women and he attempts to make us feel inferior or unneeded. He tricks us into complacent behaviors and busyness with worldly things that don't matter. And if that doesn't work, he has other tactics to try. If we aren't busy then we are told how we aren't good enough or that we don't have a role to play. Those messages of Satan's are absolutely not true. Satan is attacking the power that women can have on the movement of the Gospel.

God has always known the power women have in this gospel. We have the power to shift the focus of the women of the world by lovingly gathering them with us—to join us and giving them a place to belong.

We have been called to gather using our own spiritual gifts; to cultivate, use, and expand them to gather Israel on both sides of the veil.

Awakening your natural ability to gather.

So, this gathering is essential and the women of the Church have a special role in it. But how does this look? And how do we do it?

Michelle D. Craig, from the Young Women General Presidency, gave an amazing talk in October 2019 about listening to the Holy Ghost and finding our errands from the Lord. She referenced Alma 22:4 that says: "And Aaron said unto the king: Behold, the Spirit of

> *"We have to be different from the world and we need to be happy about it."*
> - *Rhonda Steed*

the Lord has called him another way." Applying this to our lives, Sister Craig said: "The Spirit spoke to my heart: each of us has a different mission to perform, and at times the Spirit may call us in 'another way.'"[372]

Sister Craig taught us that there are many ways for each individual covenant-keeping woman in the church to help build the kingdom.

"As His faithful disciple, you can receive personal inspiration and revelation, consistent with His commandments, that is tailored to

---

[372] Craig, Michelle D. "Spiritual Capacity," General Conference October 2019

you. You have unique missions and roles to perform in life and will be given unique guidance to fulfill them."[373]

I love that she told us directly that our paths WILL NOT look the same. Though each of us will walk paths differently, we are all headed the same direction—towards Jesus Christ.

Sister Craig went on to compare three different experiences of having to cross a large body of water. And how different those experiences looked for those who were called. Nephi was taught exactly how to build a big ship that carried his family to a new continent.[374] The brother of Jared built barges that were "tight like unto a dish"[375] with small stones for light that the Lord touched.[376] And Moses had the entire sea part so that he could lead the Israelites across on dry ground.[377]

They all had a similar problem but each had completely different paths to accomplish it. Each of them trusted what God told them to do and acted.

"The Lord is mindful of those who obey and, in the words of Nephi, will "prepare a way for [us to] accomplish the thing which he commandeth." Note that Nephi says, "a way"—not "the way.""[378]

Do we miss or dismiss personal errands from the Lord because He has prepared "a way"[379] different from the one we expect? I had my own spiritual realization about my personal role in the gathering of

[373] Ibid.
[374] 1 Nephi 17, The Book of Mormon.
[375] Ether 2, The Book of Mormon.
[376] Ether 3, The Book of Mormon.
[377] Exodus 14, Holy Bible, KJV.
[378] Craig, Michelle D. "Spiritual Capacity," General Conference October 2019
[379] Ibid.

Israel. It came to me as I was pondering how He can use me as I am to gather Israel. The Lord told me my skill of gathering is one God has given me and wants me to use to further His work on the earth.

I feel called to gather people and build relationships and to help others to do the same in their own way. The Lord has helped me develop this skill for a few years before I even knew what was happening. There was a need growing inside me that was being answered by gathering friends everywhere we lived. We would move for my husband's educational pursuits to a new province or city and each time I would work hard to gather friends and strengthen relationships. I felt drawn to do it and I have gained so much in the process of doing it.

One of the big challenges in these latter-days is how separated we get from each other physically and emotionally. We are connected more online and less in person. Satan fills our time with superficial relationships as a substitute for real relationships. He tempts us with comparing ourselves with others instead of collaborating. Comparison separates us. Collaborating connects us. True connection happens in person with friends and family and is vital for our health and emotional welfare.[380] To foster these true connections, we need to spend some time in person, getting to know each other. Dieter F. Uchdorft said, "Love is spelled T-I-M-E."[381]

I learned this as my husband and I moved our family multiple times in the first fifteen years of our marriage. These moves took us from the prairies of Alberta, Canada to the Maritimes in Nova Scotia and back again to a few different cities and communities on the prairies.

---

[380] Ortiz-Ospina, Esteban. "How Important Are Social Relations for Our Health and Well-Being?" *Our World in Data*, 17 Jan. 2019, ourworldindata.org/social-relations-health-and-well-being.
[381] Uchtdorf, Dieter F. "Of Things That Matter Most," General Conference October 2010

Every time we have moved, I would end up complaining to my husband about my lack of friends and every time he'd respond, "give it a year." And he was right, usually after a year I had found my place. On one of our moves, we felt directed even to the specific home we were moving into. We both knew that we were called to buy that home specifically for the ward it was in.

On our first Sunday, I thought I'd be able to figure out why we were there and who we were there for. After two months, I still hadn't found my way into a group of friends and I was feeling lost and lonely. It's not that people weren't nice to me, because they were. But I didn't have any feeling towards the beginning of strong relationships or even people I was supposed to be spending time with. And I was aching to be actually seen and known—to connect with other women in a way that would bless both of us.

I got a blessing from my husband about finding my place. In the blessing I was told it was important to recognize that all people have things to contribute and there was good in all people. I needed to focus on building relationships.

In a general conference address in 2019, Stephen W. Owen said something that stuck out so loud to me: "Never underestimate the strength that comes from gathering with others who are also trying to be strong."[382]

I have found that power in my own life. In times I have been weighed down, I have found connection and support through gathering. For example, in every ward we have moved into I have found a group of like-minded women in Relief Society. As well as our family has found friendships for children in the wards. It has

---

[382] Owen, Stephen W. "Be Faithful, Not Fearless," General Conference November 2019

always taken some work on our part to build those relationships, but we have always been rewarded for our effort.

The changes in the church to ministering from visiting teaching is a way to encourage us to build close, meaningful relationships with each other. The Lord wants us to reach out and minister in a one-on-one way. Jean B. Bingham, Relief Society General President talked about how ministering can vary in the way it looks. What you actually do can vary from going on walks to playing games. And how you do it can vary from visiting in person or texting. You can share a scripture or quote from a conference talk or discuss a gospel question. In the end she summed it up with a powerful line: "It looks like becoming part of someone's life and caring about him or her."[383]

When we truly care about others, we will invite them into our lives and have them become part of our lives.

I listened and obeyed by bringing people into our home. Over the next eight months I invited all kinds of new people over. Did I magically find my place and my people? Nope. When the first few didn't bloom into close friendships I started counting. I had 50 people into our home. From those 50, only one person reciprocated the invitation. But I didn't let that deter me. I kept on inviting and the blessings of that experience were huge. I worked hard inviting and introducing myself over and over. Putting myself out there again and again so that I could find those who were looking to make friendships too.

Eventually I gathered a group of women who also craved connection. With these women, we were able to change the feeling in the ward to one of connection and strength. Many of the strong friendships I formed in that ward are still in my life today, blessing me even though many of them don't live in the same community. Some of these dear friends have told me that *they learned how to gather* from our time together.

More often than not, people are willing and wanting to connect. Remember back when you were little, playing at the park, and noticed a new kid. That kid had red shoes on and you loved red. So, you said, "Hey nice shoes, wanna play?" And then you had a new friend. Somehow, we lose that ability when we age. Don't most of us love it if someone new asks us to hang out or play? I do! It's hard to be the one to make the first step—to be the one inviting instead of the one invited.

Broadening Our Definition of Gathering

Gathering for some people comes more naturally. That is okay. You can work within your own natural abilities, likes and skills and grow and develop new skills, too. So, how can you figure out the right way to gather people that will work for you? Here are a few things to keep in mind that can help make it easier. Here are some ideas that may help you get started or expand your gathering skills.

1. **Start out simple**. Don't complicate it. Start with one person that you can reach out to. If you don't know who, then pray and Heavenly Father will tell you who and how to reach out.

   a. Just invite a few friends over and try inviting someone new so that you all can get to know them. You don't have to make it complicated at all. Simple gatherings that have a great feeling do just as much good as an intense gathering with tons of fancy frills.

---

[383] Bingham, Jean B. "Ministering as the Savior Does," General Conference April 2018

b. You might ask a good friend to something you already have planned with your family. This may help you ease into gathering.

c. Or invite one *new* friend or family to something you already planned to do.

d. Keeping the gathering small and informal may increase your comfort level.

e. Maybe you love hosting people in your home. Cool, do it. Maybe that sounds terrifying, that's okay. Get a friend who wants to host at her home or meet at the park.

f. As your comfort level increases, you can branch out into new and exciting ways of gathering by increasing your numbers, varying the people you include and the type of activity you plan.

Do it how it works for you: Think about what you enjoy doing that could easily include someone else. Or, if there is something you always wanted to try doing, then plan it so it will work with someone else included. Here are some variations. Which groupings appeal to you?

a. With kids, without kids, with husbands, without husbands.

b. Big gatherings, small gatherings

c. Strictly women or mixed,

d. The same age as you and your family, older, seniors, newlyweds

e. Adults only, teen-agers only, children only, or everyone on your street.

All these variations are still gathering people and building the kingdom within your sphere of influence. Each of our roles in the Gathering of Israel is going to look so different. All provide a way for the Lord to work through us to accomplish His purposes.

3. **Use food creatively**. Everybody loves food. It's an easy way to bond with others. I have found that people who might not let you in to minister would probably go out to eat or come over for lunch. It has been one of the best ways of gathering in homes that I have found. It may be easier to form a friend or get a smile with a loaf of something tasty in your hands. Here are some more ideas for using food creatively.

   a. People's eyes really light up when they see a beautiful charcuterie board set out.

   b. It can be fun to just invite people over for dessert, rather than a whole meal! I know I love it when someone invites me over to try a new dessert. And you could even share the recipe!

   c. You can make the food or you can stop at the store and pick some up. Doesn't matter. (Remember... keep it simple.) There are so many things available at the store that can make food at a gathering easy.

   d. Do you have a special family tradition? Invite someone to share that tradition with you and your family.

   1. **Gathering has endless options.** Here are some ideas to get your mind going.

   a. Go to the park.

   b. Sit around a fire in your backyard.

   c. Send out a text with a special message, scripture or quote.

   d. Make a phone call just to say hi!

   e. Gather new moms together and help them learn how to make baby food.

   f. Start a walking group that meets once a month.

   g. Invite teenagers over for a pizza night.

   h. Gather your children around you and teach them, even if they have a friend over.

   i. Host a Friday morning brunch.

   j. Let all the kids run around your house while the ladies in Primary actually get to interact with people from your ward.

k. Form a book club and invite women to come even if they haven't read the book.

l. Have a potluck lunch and recipe exchange

m. Do you love bread? Me, too! Let's be bread friends and trade recipes.

n. Do you love music? Me, too! Come to this live music concert we're hosting at my house on Friday.

4. **Stay focused on connecting.** Either simple or fancy or anything in between can work when you have a good feeling. Remember it's more about connecting with others in meaningful ways. What really truly matters in the idea of gathering people is to make them feel comfortable and loved. All the other details are like a nice cherry on top of the sundae.

Find something you have in common with someone else and find a way to capitalize on it as you prepare to gather. Anything can be used to make a connection. People connect over similarities all the time. It's the same as when we were kids and we made friendships over cute red shoes. We're all just taller (probably) and older (definitely).

Barbara B. Smith, a past General Relief Society President said:

"There is no one more important than the individual." The individual human being is the most important entity on the face of the earth. The child of God is the one thing in mortality that was coexistent as an intelligence with God himself."[384]

We know this fact: that it always comes down to the individual. We see it in the temple, in the way we participate in ordinances, in the

---

[384] Smith, Barbara B. "Roots and Wings." *BYU Speeches*, 9 Feb. 1978, speeches.byu.edu/talks/barbara-b-smith/roots-wings/.

way our prayers are answered. God comes to each of us individually—just like we need to come to Him. Our Heavenly Father has told us we need to help save our fellow heavenly siblings and we need to do it one-by-one.

Increasing Our Capacity to Gather

> "*Though each of us will walk paths differently, we are all headed the same direction - towards Jesus Christ.*"
> — Rhonda Steed

As I was studying Nephi recently, I learned something about him. He was a builder. It says in 2 Nephi 5:15: "I did teach my people to build buildings and to work in all manner of wood…" and they used those skills to build a temple.[385]

Nephi was not always a temple builder. In fact, years earlier when their family was travelling through the wilderness away from Jerusalem, he did his first building. And it was a bow so that they could eat.[386] He started with building a bow. Then when they got to the land Bountiful where the Lord commanded them to cross, Nephi learned to build a boat.[387] There is a big difference between building a bow and building a boat or a temple.

The Lord taught him how to build all of those things to fulfill a need they had. The Lord can do this with each of us in our lives. And just like Nephi didn't know he would one day be building a boat to carry his family across an ocean, we might not know what the Lord will need us to do in the future.

---

[385] 2 Nephi 5:16, The Book of Mormon.
[386] 1 Nephi 16, The Book of Mormon.
[387] 1 Nephi 17, The Book of Mormon.

Whether we choose to have a group of three or a group of 25, it doesn't matter. Just get people together and let them develop relationships and connect. When we position ourselves in the right places with the right people, God can use those opportunities to bless lives. Start with the people you are comfortable with and then expand your circle to invite those who are lonely or new.

One of the stories in the Book of Mormon that I love talks about a woman and an impromptu gathering. In Alma, chapter 19, we read about the amazing conversion of Lamoni and his household where, after being taught the gospel, they fall into a trance as though they are dead and have angelic visitors. While this is happening, a faithful woman named Abish is preserved as a witness. She is a faithful servant in the household of the king. In verse 16, it says there was "...one of the Lamanitish women, whose name was Abish, she, having been converted unto the Lord for many years, on account of a remarkable vision of her father."

This woman was placed there for this moment. She saw what was happening as an opportunity to teach others. Abish saw a need and got to work, quickly gathering people. In verse 17 it says:

"...she knew that it was the power of God; and supposing that this opportunity, by making known unto the people what had happened among them, that by beholding this scene it would cause them to believe in the power of God, therefore she ran forth from house to house, making it known unto the people."

Abish noticed something special and important was happening. She saw and then acted upon what she saw by running and gathering as many people as possible. However, the gathering did not work the way she expected. Even when she did what she was supposed to do, contention still broke out; and Abish broke down into tears. Verse 28 goes on to say:

"And thus, the contention began to be exceedingly sharp among them. And while they were thus contending, the woman servant who had caused the multitude to be gathered together came, and when she saw the contention which was among the multitude she was exceedingly sorrowful, even unto tears."

This faithful woman was living her life and was where she was supposed to be. She had done what she was inspired to do. She simply acted.

Remember my son Eli? How his castle-building didn't turn out the way he expected? Eli had a great attitude about it and just kept working, moving on to a new location and carrying on his work. He didn't dwell on things that kept interrupting him or having to change his plan. Instead he just got to work over and over again with complete joy.

After Abish felt she had failed, a wonderful spiritual experience still took place. Verse 29 says:

"And it came to pass that she went and took the queen by the hand, that perhaps she might raise her from the ground; and as soon as she touched her hand she arose and stood upon her feet, and cried with a loud voice, saying: O blessed Jesus, who has saved me from an awful hell! O blessed God, have mercy on this people!"

The queen and all the others awoke and testified. Some did not believe and left, but there were many people who were converted to the gospel. Their lives *were* changed by this gathering.

One of the great lessons I get from the story of Abish is that even if my gatherings might not go how I plan, God can still work wonders. He can touch lives and accomplish whatever things He has planned because it is His work. Sometimes I think we forget who's work this really is. I believe the prophet when he said, "…this gathering is *the greatest* challenge, *the greatest* cause, and *the greatest* work on earth today"!"[388] It is a cause that desperately needs women, because "women shape the future."[389] Not only do I believe this but I also believe that God will help me as I go about trying to gather His children. I certainly have been discouraged when things didn't go as I planned. I have also had many experiences with gathering people and realized that God had a better outcome than I had imagined.

If Heavenly Father can create worlds without numbers and help Moses walk through the Red Sea on dry ground,[390] why would I doubt His ability to help me as I try to help Him in his work and glory? I know without a doubt that God loves all of His children. There are no catches to that statement. He loves us because He is good and He will always love us no matter what. God loves those within the gospel fold, and all of those not in it, as well. Carole M. Stephens, from the Relief Society General Presidency said, "Do you know deep in your heart that your Heavenly Father loves you and desires you and those you love to be with Him?"[391]

You have the power to change the world

God feels deep love for all his children. He desperately wants to save all of them. But He involves us in His work and invites us to use our hands and our hearts on this earth.

---

[388] Nelson, Russell M. "Sisters' Participation in the Gathering of Israel," General Conference October 2018
[389] Ibid.
[390] Exodus 14, Holy Bible, KJV.
[391] Stephens, Carole M. "The Family is of God," General Conference April 2015

Barbara B. Smith gave great advice to the women of the church in 1979: "Value yourself and be about your Father's business for your personal exaltation, and then love your fellow men so much that you will help them do the same."[392] If we act out of love, like Abish did, then we will be able to help others find Jesus Christ. She invited others to come and see so they could personally experience the miracle of conversion. We can help those who are baptized in our faith and those who walk a different path. All of us need strengthening. All of us need connection and a place to feel loved. All of us need to be gathered.

Often, we get promptings to reach out to others: to help, to serve, to comfort. Have you ever felt one of those? God sends us little nudges to encourage us to help His children around us. Spencer W. Kimball said: "God does notice us, and he watches over us. But it is usually through another person that he meets our needs."[393] God uses us, if we are willing, to reach His children wherever we are and wherever they are. Since He knows what we are good at, and our abilities, He can use us *as we are* to help in His cause. Knowing that God is aware of all of His children helps us to trust His ability to use us for good.

Donna Smith Packer, wife of Boyd K. Packer said: "We can't go too far astray if we, on bended knee, place a call to our Heavenly Father's home twice a day. We will receive the expected help, assurance, and peace of mind."[394] If we pray and ask, Heavenly Father *will* tell us who, how and when to gather those around us.

---

[392] Smith, Barbara B. "Roots and Wings." *BYU Speeches*, 9 Feb. 1978, speeches.byu.edu/talks/barbara-b-smith/roots-wings/.

[393] Kimball, Spencer W. "Small Acts of Service." *The Church of Jesus Christ of Latter-Day Saints*, Dec. 1974, www.churchofjesuschrist.org/study/ensign/1974/12/small-acts-of-service?lang=eng.

[394] Packer, Donna Smith. "Her Calling-Her Blessing." *BYU Speeches*, 29 Apr. 2004, speeches.byu.edu/talks/donna-smith-packer/calling-blessing-2/.

As we gather other children of God into our homes and lives, we will have opportunities to bless them, expand our circles, and bring others closer to Jesus Christ. This gathering does not have an exact formula to follow. But instead it is distinct to each one of us, and our lives. This gathering looks like mom's groups and walking clubs. It looks like dinner clubs and Friday night pizza parties with teenagers. Maybe you are really great at gathering large groups of women into your home. If so—run with it. Maybe you are really great at small groups of children and helping them feel loved and a part of things. Great. Do it. In whatever way you feel called to gather any of the children of the world, God invites you to. Each of us is so needed in this gathering process.

Jesus Christ ministered one-by-one while He was on the earth. And it is how He gathers us now. The same is true for us. We can trust Him to teach us how to gather, as He does with our own skills and our own lives. Know that God sees our skills, needs and abilities, as well as all those around us. Being able to see all of us for who we really are, He can weave our lives together in meaningful ways.

> *"Each of our roles in the Gathering of Israel is going to look so different. All provide a way for the Lord to work through us to accomplish His purposes."*
> - *Rhonda Steed*

Donna Smith Packer talked about how this knowledge of God seeing us for who we are can help us in our daily lives by giving us confidence and courage.

"We can yield our agency to the Lord and let him manage our lives. I know it requires faith to do this, but our divine nature (as women) gives us that strength, and we find joy in our commitment and our duty."[395]

Because the Lord loves us, understands us, He will bless us for our desires and efforts.

The more we allow others into our homes and build relationships with others, the "good women of the world"[396] will actually be able to see the "women of the Church reflect righteousness and articulateness in their lives."[397] Then we will draw them to us and help them find the love of Jesus Christ in their lives because of who we are. We don't need to be anyone else—just ourselves—God will use us.

Bonnie H. Cordon, Young Women General President, said: "Whether our sheep are strong or weak, rejoicing or in anguish, we can make certain that no one walks alone. We can love them wherever they are spiritually and offer support and encouragement for the next step forward."[398]

Gathering women into your home is a wonderful way to minister to the "strong or weak, rejoicing or in anguish."[399] I believe so strongly that we need each other. And as we gather people around us, we will find strength in our numbers—we will find a place for all of God's children.

Another lesson from Eli building his castles in the sand in Nova Scotia is that we sometimes will have to pick up our tools and move

---

[395] Ibid.
[396] Kimball, Spencer W. "The Role of Righteous Women," General Conference October 1979
[397] Ibid.
[398] Cordon, Bonnie H. "Becoming a Shepard," General Conference October 2018
[399] Ibid.

where we work: to a different calling, a different group of people, to a different role, to minister to a different person. The ocean water is like God directing us to move somewhere else. You work in one place and then you'll get up, pick up your treasured talents and skills and work in a different place.

"Begin by being a good neighbor and a good friend. Set an example of righteousness and kindness. Let your smile radiate love, peace, and happiness. Live a gospel-centered life,"[400] said Silvia H. Allred, Relief Society General Presidency.

Allow people into your life by gathering them wherever you are. They'll be able to feel when you truly mean it—that feeling that someone is interested in being their true friend is what will make the difference. When God wants us to be in someone's life the Spirit will touch them and they will see the light of the Gospel shining in our lives. That is how we will truly gather them with us.

Just like Eli building sandcastles that were washed away, the work we do might not be seen by others. In fact, it probably won't be seen by others. It will be small simple things that God needs done. But despite it being unseen or intense, we can have joy in knowing we are doing what God called us to do. We don't have to see any evidence or results of our work. In the end we can look back with joy, see that we were moved by the Lord, knowing we did what God called us to do. True joy comes from knowing that Jesus Christ has provided a way for all of us to return to live with Him and helping others know that too. So, as we gather the people together around us, let that be the underlying purpose so that it can guide how and what we do to gather. Let it guide our interactions with our children, our extended family, our neighbors and even strangers.

---

[400] Allred, Sylvia H. "Go Ye Therefore," General Conference October 2008

Remember what the prophet said?

"This gathering is *"the greatest* challenge, *the greatest* cause, and *the greatest* work on earth today"*! It is a cause that desperately needs women, because women shape the future."[401]

We've been called to gather. I'm up for it, are you?

---

[401] Nelson, Russell M. "Sisters' Participation in the Gathering of Israel," General Conference October 2018

*We have the power to
shift the focus of the
women of the world by
lovingly gathering them
with us – to join us
and giving them a
place to belong.*

– Rhonda Steed –

—11—
Kay West

You Are a Mountain Mover

She sat next to me and I was excited. This beautiful, amazing woman! I was thrilled to get to know her, because she was someone I admired and looked up to.

Then she softly whispered, "I can't believe I am in the presence of these Mountain Movers."

I was taken aback. Here was a woman I distinctly saw as a mountain mover, who clearly did not see herself as one.

How often are we guilty of doing that to ourselves?

I can recall times in my life where I have felt alone, unnoticed by a world full of commotion flying past me at breakneck speed. I remember moments where I have been brought low before a mountain I knew I had to climb, but unsure hand and foot holds left me guessing how, or where to even begin. I remember paths that took me to places of doubt, fear, and insecurity, abandoning me to call out "*why me?*" with seemingly no reply.

And I remember hope.

A peace and light.

A love and understanding.

A knowledge and faith in Christ.

And that is what will help us to not only climb mountains, but move them!

It was my parents that first showed me the possibility of moving personal mountains. My father's earliest childhood memories are of World War II. One day, he was playing with his little sister and other children in the street. The warning sirens suddenly blared, screaming at them all to take cover in the closest bomb shelter. The next day they would return again because "they always did."

One particular day, as the shells dropped my father and aunt ran to the shelter in a nearby farmer's field. My father explained that these makeshift shelters were cold cellars—root vegetable storage that were dugout in the farmer's fields. My father told me he would dive over and under people, pulling my aunt along behind him to get to the very back corner so they could hide behind everyone else. That day, when the sirens fell silent, my father and aunt went looking for their friends. They were in a shelter down the road from where they had been playing earlier. The brother and sister were holding each other tight, completely blackened by the bombs that had fallen. Their friends would no longer be able to play with them.

My father, due to poverty after the war, at the age of 14 had to begin taking care of himself and put himself through evening school by working in a metal factory by day. The factory provided gloves that protected the workers' hands and came to their wrists. To this day, my father's arms bear the scars where the molten metal splashed him.

Between work and school, the daily path my father traveled took him past the "Mormon missionaries" who were standing on street corners preaching the message of the restored gospel of Jesus Christ. My father listened to them, was soon converted, and served a service mission in Japan where he labored in the construction of church buildings. My mother was the first person baptized in the church my father helped build. My parents had a civil marriage in Japan, traveled to Hawaii where they were sealed in the Hawaiian Temple, and from there immigrated to Canada without family, money, knowledge of the language or culture, and almost no belongings.

One of my fondest childhood memories is when my parents would gather my four sisters and me in the living room around the coffee table. This is where my father would tell us his "life stories." My mother paints with oils and brushes, my father draws with pencil and charcoal, and my father's Life Stories involved him bringing stories to life through his sketches. The records left behind are the hand-drawn images of his life growing up during and after the war in Japan.

In my father's words, his father was a "drunkard." My father recalls that although my grandfather was often intoxicated, he would tell him the funniest stories of his travels in the mountains. I believe this is how my father's imagination was sparked, and how he became a great storyteller himself.

One particular life story my father would tell us was a Japanese parable that he made up.

I would like to share his parable with you:

In a small Japanese village nestled in the mountains, there stood a tall, steep, sheer cliff mountain that cast its shadow over the village. As a rite of passage, when the young boys in the village came of age they would climb that mountain and become men. They would accomplish this great task, learn lessons, and gain valuable knowledge.

The day for one young boy fast approached and with each passing day, he became more excited. Finally, the day arrived, and the boy awoke early in the morning, too eager to sleep any longer. A note from his father was on the table, it asked him not to leave until after his father was awake. Impatient to get on his way, he did not do this and instead left a note saying he had gone.

He began his journey and the long climb. The sun began to rise, and this young man had not made it very far, only about a quarter of the way. By noon, the sun beat down on him, wearying him. And still, he had so much farther to go. As the afternoon sun began to descend, and the sky hinted at the oncoming darkness, the boy began to worry. He was still so far from the top. Finally, at the end of the third day, the boy made it to the top.

With no food and very little water left, he was surprised to see a basket of fresh food, water, and a note with his name on it.

He was even more surprised to find it was a note from his father.

"Son, I have waited for you each day, hoping to see you. If you had just waited for me, I could have shown you the way. Climbing the mountain is not all that makes you a man. It is also the lessons you learn along the way. There is an easier way. I wanted to show you that way."

Sure enough, following his father's directions, the boy found the other way. Still steep and difficult, but not so treacherous. Indeed, it would still prove a great challenge to climb, a challenge that would teach valuable lessons and provide knowledge. But the climb could be made in a single day, and it was the climb he knew he was meant to take.

My father's parable has always stuck with me because in life we all face mountains we need to climb. Our mountains are an opportunity for character building, progression, learning, and growth. From the front, our mountains may seem daunting, menacing, and even insurmountable. But, just as in my father's parable, maybe we just need to take a different approach. Maybe get a little help along our way, both of the heavenly and earthly kind. Then our mountains become possible and achievable no matter how difficult the climb ahead.

I have journeyed through racism, together with my husband we have journeyed through infertility and I have had miscarriages and a d-and-c. We adopted our two children (both from birth), had a failed adoption, and our daughter has multiple physical and mental special needs.

These experiences have humbled me and brought me, sobbing, to my knees. They have also brought me to key switchbacks when I needed them, and then onto paths that diverged into even more unknown and steep climbs. I have found myself asking why, being angry, and frustrated, trying to gain understanding when at times the experience was the only lesson I needed.

Just like you, I too know what it feels like when you face mountains that at first glance may seem too difficult to climb. If you have ever hiked a steep mountain trail, you know that there are points called switchbacks that offer some relief to those climbing. These switchbacks are 180° turns along the path, allowing hikers to climb up the side of the mountain, back and forth at a steady incline, instead of climbing in a line straight up the mountain. One hope-filled truth for us is that we too have spiritual switchbacks that will help ease our climb.

I would like to share 6 switchbacks with you.

Switchback One: Never doubt your own abilities.

As I have shared, my parents immigrated to Canada with almost nothing. When they arrived they found work in the day, took evening classes to learn English, and worked as janitors at night. They faced years of hardships and racism in the community and within their own church family. As new converts in a new land, I cannot begin to imagine how truly alone they must have felt.

> *"If we are placed in human orbits to illuminate, then it is up to us to learn why we have crossed paths with certain individuals."*
> - Kay West

However, years later, they are doing so much good for so many individuals and families. Through their consistent hard work, my father became a Journeyman Carpenter, as well as the President and CEO of his own company. My mother earned her Bachelor's degree in Business when my sisters and I were young, and then opened one of the largest private-owned English as a Second Language (ESL) schools in Western Canada.

To take a quick look at the start of my parents' climbs; it would have been easy to assume the outcome would be difficult, maybe even unsuccessful.

Sometimes we view the beginning of our own journey up our mountain with similar eyesight. Maybe we judge that we will not be successful on our climb, and we may even consider one failure to be the end of our climb altogether. But might I share this beautiful reminder from President Monson? You do not need to "pray for tasks equal to your abilities, but pray for abilities equal to your tasks.

Then the performance of your tasks will be no miracle, but you will be the miracle."[402]

The beginning of your climb is just that; it's the place you start.

Women who you recognize as women, who have conquered and moved their mountains, began their climb at exactly the same place you do.

At the foot of a mountain.

There is no need to delay your climb. "Procrastination wears us out…"[403] If you try to wait for the perfect moment to start your ascent, the *right* time to begin might pass you by.

Each woman who stands at the foot of her mountain has worry and doubt, and each begins her climb with uncertainty. You are the same as every successful woman who has ever reached her summit. The same as any woman who you have ever seen move mountains. And you have the knowledge that you will be the miracle because you have everything you need within you if you just ask. I know this is true, a prophet of God told me it is.

Switchback Two: Our paths cross so we may lift one another.

A couple of years ago I was invited to attend an event. The organizer explained he had attended a conference where the speaker told everyone to get to know the person sitting next to them. In his case, the person next to him was an older widow and he was pretty sure he had nothing in common with her. But the exercise was to get to know her, so he did. They became friends, and she even spent time with him and his family.

A few years later, the new company he was building was facing foreclosure. This woman he had become friends with asked him if he

---

Monson, Thomas S. "Three Goals to Guide You," General Conference October 2007
[403] Hinckley, Marjorie Pay. "Just Do What Needs to Be Done." *BYU Speeches*, 11 Apr. 2000, speeches.byu.edu/talks/marjorie-pay-hinckley/just-needs-done/.

would let her be an investor in his company. It turned out that the widow he could have ignored because they had "nothing in common," had the means that would end up saving his company and help make it the success it is today. This would not have been possible if he had not taken the time to get to know her. His point was, you just never know who the person standing in front of you will turn out to be.

Have you ever met someone, but because you felt there was no "connection" or you had "nothing in common" with them you didn't make too great an effort to get to know them? Or maybe you were the one someone did not make an effort to get to know?

Neal A. Maxwell said: "Recall the new star that announced the birth at Bethlehem? It was in its precise orbit long before it so shone. We are likewise placed in human orbits to illuminate."[404]

Have you ever thought about this? I have! I think if Heavenly Father knows the precise orbit of a single star, the fall of a single sparrow, or the growth of one blade of grass, then He knows who we need to cross paths with in life. Isn't it a beautiful thought? To think we cross paths with one another by Divine design? Think about the individuals you have met in your life. People you feel like you are meant to know, or maybe even knew before this life.

If we are placed in human orbits to illuminate, then it is up to us to learn why we have crossed paths with certain individuals. To discover how we can learn and grow from the connections we make with them. Whether we are to lift that person or they are meant to lift us. Or, even better, maybe we are to lift one another and grow together!

A favorite quote from C.S. Lewis shares, "There are no ordinary people. You have never talked to a mere mortal."[405] C.S. Lewis

---

[404] Maxwell, Neal A. "Encircled in the Arms of His Love," General Conference October 2002

reminds us that we are all immortal, we are all individual beings of Divine Heritage. He cautions us that as we cross paths one with another we are helping one another to become "immortal horrors or everlasting splendours."[406]

I want to make sure that every day of my journey I am helping each person I meet become an "everlasting splendor"[407].

When we give our time to loving those around us, and to lift them on their path, we are also helping ourselves. We do not always know the individual we are helping, or what future role they might play in our lives. My parents are a perfect example of this; from the start of their climb to where they are now.

Remember the beginning of my parents' climbs in a new country? If you were to cross paths with them back then perhaps you might think they would not be able to help anyone. And now? Who knew that years later they would be in a position to help so many? And many favors were returned along their journey.

Someone on a similar climb to you may need help, and their path might bring them within arms reach of your path. If you can help them, then reach out and help in any way you can. It may not be too much farther along on your own climb that you will be the one who will need the assistance their reach can offer.

Although we do not know the reason our paths cross in life, what we do know is that we are here to become more like our Savior, in word and deed. "Our greatest performance is when we take the time to give of ourselves in love, one for another, often away from the crowd."[408]

---

[405] Lewis, C.S. The Weight of Glory. HarperOne an Imprint of HarperCollins Publishers, 2001, p.46.
[406] Ibid.
[407] Ibid.
[408] Kapp, Ardeth G. "That We May Prepare to Do Our Part - Ardeth G. Kapp." *BYU Speeches*, 4 June 1989, speeches.byu.edu/talks/ardeth-g-kapp/may-prepare-part/.

This is what He did and does for each of us.

We may find we are climbing a mountain because of the choices of others or because of the consequences and circumstances of everyday life. And sometimes we climb because we feel called to climb. No matter how we come to climb each mountain, we know that "The Lord has laid high responsibilities upon us."[409] In a meeting in which Eliza R. Snow was in attendance, a sister made this comment: "It is uphill business."[410] After hearing this, Eliza elaborated on this sister's statement and shared, "It *is* uphill. And if you continue, you will attain to something much higher than those who go downhill."[411]

Whatever mountain you feel called to tackle, whatever trial you will face, it will be uphill, because with every mountain there is a climb. Our climbs to fulfill our missions or to overcome struggles—whatever they may be—are upward, but that does not mean that we need to struggle unnecessarily by climbing alone.

When we look around and see others climbing near us, recognizing we are all headed to the same summit, then working together helps us attain that "something much higher."[412]

I believe it is one reason our paths intersect with others, for however limited or lengthy a time, to help lift each other along the way. Uphill business is hard for everyone, and so we all know a little of what it is to lend a helping hand or take one when extended.

Switchback Three: Keep taking small, simple, and faithful steps forward.

---

[409] Eliza R. Snow, "An Elevation so High Above the Ordinary," *At the Pulpit: 185 years of Discourses by Latter-day Saint Women*, Intellectual Reserve, Inc., 2017, p.56. Emphasis added.
[410] Ibid.
[411] Ibid.
[412] Ibid.

The past few years there has been a recognizable hastening in God's plan for His Church. We have seen organizational and policy changes revealed at what seems an accelerated rate. The revelations received and implemented are almost overwhelming when we think about it as one great whole. Sometimes I feel like I am running just to keep up!

When I take a moment; when I stop running and break down each direction given individually, I can see it is not one giant change all at once. We have received instruction as the Lord has promised He would give it to us; little by little.

> *For behold, thus saith the Lord God: I will give unto the children of men line upon line, precept upon precept, here a little and there a little; and blessed are those who hearken unto my precepts, and lend an ear unto my counsel, for they shall learn wisdom; for unto him that receiveth I will give more.*[413]

I am grateful that in all ways and in all things the Lord does for us, change does not occur all at once; but line upon line, in the Lord's time and in the Lord's way. This is one way He blesses us with the knowledge we need to keep moving forward.

It's important to remember that just as the Lord gives us instruction, little by little, likewise we must keep our pace moving forward in the same manner with Him. Little by little, step by step. Then we won't need to catch our breath from running so hard to keep up.

I love to study the ever-stalwart example of Nephi in the Book of Mormon. His family had been traveling in the wilderness for some time, and the Lord led them in "the most fertile parts of the wilderness"[414] so they could obtain food for their families. After traveling for so long, all of their bows were rendered useless, including Nephi's steel bow. When Nephi's bow broke, everyone

---

[413] 2 Nephi 28:30, The Book of Mormon.
[414] 1 Nephi 16:14, The Book of Mormon.

was angry. Instead of doing anything about it, they all murmur. The exception, of course, was Nephi, who made a new bow and arrow. He then went to see his father and asked where he should go hunting for food. Lehi prayed, was chastened by the Lord, and repented of his murmuring. Then he received direction from the Lord about where Nephi could obtain food. "And it came to pass that I, Nephi, did go forth up into the top of the mountain, according to the directions which were given upon the ball."[415]

When we think about this story, we often ponder why no one else thought to make a weapon to obtain food. Sometimes we contemplate how even Lehi murmured and then was chastened by the Lord. We may wonder at how Nephi learned that the Liahona worked according to their faith and obedience. Or maybe we marvel at how the Lord can make great even our small efforts.

There is a lesson I learned from this story that is not the "typical" lesson. When everyone is choosing to complain, Nephi not only makes a new bow and asks where to get food, but the answer he receives is to "go forth up into the top of the mountain."[416]

That's right, the answer Nephi received to overcome the problem was to climb a mountain.

When everyone else was choosing to stop taking any steps at all, Nephi chose to continue taking small and simple steps forward and then was sent to take many more faithful steps up a mountain. I am sure Nephi was just as tired and hungry as his family. Yet instead of resting, he faithfully continued on. Tired, hungry, and dealing with a whole group of extended families that were tired and hungry, he said, "...I, Nephi, did go forth up into the top of the mountain..."[417]

---

[415] 1 Nephi 16:30, The Book of Mormon.
[416] Ibid.
[417] Ibid.

I don't think anyone would consider going to the top of the mountain to obtain food as an easy answer. But because of Nephi's willing faithfulness to continue trying, a path did open to him. Answers came and he was able to relieve the suffering, doubt, and fear the others were feeling. He could have said it was too much even for him to bear. But instead, he moved forward with faith even when those faithful steps forward meant he had to climb a mountain.

The Lord provides us answers line upon line and we must progress forward line upon line. To me, this means taking small, simple, and faithful steps forward. Perhaps, like Nephi, those faithful steps forward will bring us to another mountain. Then there may be times where we have to take a

> *"God does not delegate our prayers to anyone else. He hears each and every prayer, and He answers them."*
> *- Kay West*

step or two backward. That is when we have the opportunity to stop, ask the Lord for help, and continue with small and simple steps forward.

Even a tiny, faithful, baby step forward is a step forward.

Switchback Four: Obey guidance and direction given by our prophets and apostles.

Standing alone, Sister Elaine Cannon was waiting for the elevator when two security officers held some doors open and President Kimball walked through. Unsure if she should get on the elevator with him, she waited outside the elevator thinking to take the next one. President Kimball smiled at her and said good morning. She smiled back and responded with her own morning greeting. He then asked if she was going to get on the elevator, to which she responded she wasn't sure if she should. She shares this experience in a general conference address:

And [President Kimball] said, "Aren't you going up?" And I said, "Yes." And he said, "Well, tell me, how do you intend to get there?"[418]

Over the years our prophets have extended us many invitations. Invitations that will indeed help us go up if we choose to get on board with him and go, because we know that is where our prophet is going—up.

We are a worldwide sisterhood of women, each of diverse ethnic and cultural backgrounds, in different seasons of life, and involved in various trials and individual distinct joys. We are also covenant women who try to follow the Lord and the counsel of our living prophets and apostles. What a blessing it is to have them lead us and guide us in these latter-days! If we will listen to them and diligently obey, then our path does continue onward and upward even during difficult climbs.

We are part of a worldwide sisterhood and we live in an exciting time where the voices of women are stronger than ever. Our prophets and apostles have asked us women to stand up and to stand apart from the world. They want us to raise our combined voices against the evils of the day and to shine our light for the world to see. We may not always agree or understand right away, we may also have questions, but we can take heart and follow this simple, true declaration from Marjorie Pay Hinckley who said, "First I obey, then I understand."[419]

---

[418] Cannon, Elaine S. "If We Want to Go Up, We Have to Get On," General Conference October 1978

[419] Burton, Linda K. "Priesthood Power-Available to All," *Ensign*, June 2014, www.churchofjesuschrist.org/study/ensign/2014/06/priesthood-power-available-to-all?lang=eng.

We love, support, and sustain our prophets and apostles. We are so grateful to have them to lead and guide us through complicated and troubling times.

"Especially in times of discouragement, trials, and tests, leaders will help us, carry our burdens, and believe in us when we may otherwise not even believe in ourselves. Obedience is the key that unlocks the door and sets us free."[420]

When there is so much noise in the world, we can find peace in their words, because we know they speak with and for the Lord. We also know "... our most crucial work lies ahead as we join with our priesthood leaders to help move the kingdom of God forward."[421]

As we heed their guidance and direction, we will not only find the comfort and answers we seek, but we will find ourselves as instruments in the Lord's Hands. In doing so, we will be going up and that is the best direction to be going if we want to make it to the top of our mountains.

Switchback Five: Know you are a daughter of God with divine purpose and potential.

I remember early mornings seeing my father studying his scriptures at the table before work. I remember finding my mother kneeling at her bedside as I was searching for her, needing something a little girl would need from her mother. My parents' quiet examples were often of selfless service, turning the other cheek, visiting those in the hospital or those who were sick and elderly. The strength of my testimony grew over the years as I watched my parents bring many students from my mom's school to the knowledge of the gospel of Jesus Christ simply through their constant, faithful, and loving examples.

---

[420] Kapp, Ardeth G. "Your Inheritance: Secure or in Jeopardy?" *BYU Speeches*, 1 Feb. 1987, speeches.byu.edu/talks/ardeth-g-kapp/inheritance-secure-jeopardy/.
[421] Smoot, Mary E. "We Are Instruments in the Hands of God," General Conference October 2000

Their hardships did not stop them from knowing who their Heavenly Father was. They also knew who their Savior was and all that He had done for them. Having this knowledge meant they could endure their difficult climbs.

And this became another valuable lesson in my life.

I didn't know my grandparents, cousins, aunts, or uncles growing up. They lived in Japan and I never had the opportunity to meet them. I have met my maternal grandmother once, and a few aunts and uncles also once or twice. I did not know any relatives other than my pioneer parents who trekked a new path over many mountains for our little family. I remember realizing I was different from those around me who visited their grandparents on the weekends, or played with their cousins on weekdays. I remember feeling lost and unsure. My path seemed uncertain because I had no understanding of my heritage. My foundation. Where did I come from? What was my worth?

Our Heavenly Father is a master delegator, but there are three things He does not delegate:

1. His fatherhood. He is the literal Father of the human family.
2. His love. He is concerned for the welfare of all mankind.
3. His interest in us. He personally hears and answers our prayers.[422]

God does not delegate our prayers to anyone else. He hears each and every prayer, and He answers them. If we want to know who we are, we can go to Him and ask Him. And because He is concerned with our welfare and the climbs we have in this life, He will answer our prayers.

During my years of infertility and miscarriage, I struggled a lot. I found myself constantly on my knees endeavoring to understand my

---

[422] *God. Definition of God in Bible Dictionary, Bible.* Holy Bible, KJV, The Church of Jesus Christ of Latter-day Saints version.

worth. I wanted to be a mother. My experience with infertility broke my understanding of my worth as a woman. I was supposed to be a part of this great process of creation. At least that is what I had been taught my whole life.

Loved ones around me seemed to continually be having children and I was suffering in silence. Over twenty years ago, it felt like a time in society and religious culture where infertility wasn't talked about much; and at a time where I felt broken and alone. Even with my husband, my best friend by my side, I felt alone.

I remember my husband, Brad, told me that I *could* do this on my own, but that maybe my climb would be a little rockier and steeper than it needed to be. Brad knew eventually I would lean on my Father in Heaven and gently suggested that I could turn to Him right away and it might make my climb a little easier. I did turn to my Heavenly Father—in prayer, in thought, in every deed. I tried. Eventually, we were blessed with two children, adopted from birth, 13 months apart. But there were more mountains to face. I went through a miscarriage, a d-and-c, and a failed adoption with a child we had in our home from the time she was one-week-old to one-year-old.

When our children were young, we also did respite care for foster families and would often have two or three other infants in our home. With our daughter's special needs, some days were very trying and exhausting. It was a daily challenge as I tried to learn what she needed and how to communicate with her. My husband came home from work one day, and I needed help. We had two foster infants in our home and our children were almost two and three years old. As he walked through the door, I immediately asked him for a priesthood blessing. With babies napping, and toddlers running around he gave me a priesthood blessing that changed everything.

The blessing spoke very specifically about our daughter. It said her mind was not whole and wouldn't be in this life, but that the spirit within her was perfect. All of a sudden, I understood the scripture "The worth of souls is great in the sight of God."[423] And all of a sudden, I was no longer broken.

Years before my parents had taught me the worth of each individual, and that particular priesthood blessing from my husband taught me the worth of each soul. I understood our true, divine potential. Just as in Psalms we read: "God is in the midst of her; she shall not be moved: God shall help her..."[424] We know we are the daughters of a loving God, a Heavenly Father who is there for us and who wants us to be happy and return to Him.

Our identity never changes; our identities are that we are daughters and sons of loving Heavenly Parents. But our sacred roles in life are not the same as our divine purpose in life. Let me repeat that, *your role as a wife and mother is not the same as your purpose as a daughter of God.*

Everything I had been taught growing up made me believe my purpose was to be a wife and a mother. Marrying a little later than others, and facing infertility, I couldn't understand how being a wife and mother was our only purpose. What about all those women who did not marry or have children in this life? My experiences have taught me to cherish my roles of wife and mother, and to understand they are not the only roles we may have in life.

I also came to understand and honor the equally sacred purpose of being a daughter of God. Though at times our roles and purpose intertwine, they are separate, and we are each blessed with the divine gifts and attributes we need to help us fulfill the different roles we have in life and also to achieve our purpose. This was the foundation I was missing in my life.

---

[423] Doctrine and Covenants 18:10.
[424] Psalms 46:5, Holy Bible, KJV.

I learned "a woman doesn't have to stay in the house to be in the home. Neither does a woman need to leave her home to extend her influence to others."[425]

God wants to bless us according to *His plan* for us. Not our own. Not what society or the world says is our plan. Not even what our families may think is best for us. Our Heavenly Father is there for each of us individually and wants to bless us individually according to *His perfect plan* for us.

This life is an individual journey where we are each accountable for our own actions and choices that help us return to our Heavenly Parents, and all of this is my foundation. Knowing and understanding who I am, and Whose I am.

When we talk about the refining process, we talk about how different trials and challenges—the pressures we face—can help us to learn, grow, and progress. Likewise, the trials and challenges we face help us to buff away impurities and be bright, beautiful diamonds. Instead of focusing on the trials and challenges, let us never forget the most important detail in this equation: that we are diamonds. Our clarity and brilliance may require effort so we may glow with light even in dark times. But our value, our worth, that was in place before we ever came to this earth. And it has always been priceless.

We have a loving Heavenly Father constantly holding out His hand to us. Let us take a moment and grab hold of it. Or let us be the ones to stretch out to Him because no matter how far our reach, He will always make up the difference and "reach our reaching."[18]

If you think He isn't concerned with your climb in life, then I invite you to go to Him. Speak *to* Him and *with* Him, and if you need help, *ask* Him for it. I think you may be surprised to find your climb may become a little less rocky as stones are maneuvered around, or

---

[425] Cannon, Elaine A. "Our Mighty Errand," General Conference October 1979

boulders are completely removed by a Father who *loves YOU endlessly.*

Switchback Six: Keep your focus on Jesus Christ.

A star is uncomplicated; in rudimentary terms, it is a glowing ball of hydrogen and helium. The push and pull of gases and gravity cause the star to eventually begin burning. Every star, no matter the size, has a very long life, even hundreds of billions of years. That being said, all stars also eventually begin to fade and burn out. In other words, their light goes out.

> *"Your role as a wife and mother is not the same as your purpose as a daughter of God."*
> - Kay West

"They" are always telling us to "reach for the stars." Who are *they* anyway? Stars are merely a large ball of gasses that are born and then eventually die. Thus, in essence, reaching for the stars is reaching for something that is not permanent. Reaching for something that over time will eventually fade into nothing.

We need to set our sights on and reach for something that will never die; for a light that will never fade over time or in any degree of blackness, a constant and true source of light.

The Light we must seek for is our Savior, Jesus Christ. He is the final switchback that will help us with any mountain.

"Therefore, hold up your light that it may shine unto the world. Behold I am the light which ye shall hold up – that which ye have seen me do."[426] The light we are asked to hold up for the world to

---

[426] 3 Nephi 18:24, The Book of Mormon.

see is His Light, and it shines for all.[427] Our climbs will be dark at times, but we can find light on those dark paths through Jesus Christ.

"The Lord's invitation to let our light so shine is not just about randomly waving a beam of light and making the world generally brighter. It is about focusing our light so others may see the way to Christ."[428]

Whenever I think about shining the light of Christ, I imagine viewing the world from a distance, except the world is completely black. Then I imagine a single pinprick of light shining. In the darkness, it offers light to quite a large area. Then I imagine another tiny dot of light somewhere else in the world, and then another, and another until the whole world is filled with millions of tiny specks of light.

Every single light combines to completely illuminate the entire world. To me, that is the power of the focused light of Christ. Because light, especially His Light, can be seen in any amount of darkness, but darkness completely fades away in the light.

Let us "live close to the Lord, obeying his laws. Then we shall find the light and the truth we need for that particular set of problems with which we grapple individually."[429] As we begin to focus on Christ, we will more easily begin to bring Him into the focus of the light we shine for others.

Along with His light, we also need the peace, hope, truth, understanding, love, grace, and mercy He freely gives to all who seek Him. It is possible to go through life without always needing a helping hand. But in each of our climbs for eternal salvation and exaltation, no one knows or understands us better than Him, and no one can offer us the relief and assistance we truly need except for

[427] Matthew 5:14-16, Holy Bible, KJV; 3 Nephi 18:24, The Book of Mormon.
[428] Cordon, Bonnie H. "That They May See," General Conference April 2020
[429] Smith, Barbara B. "Women's Greatest Challenge," General Conference October 1978

Him. God's eternal plan of happiness is a climb achieved only through Christ.

We know Jesus Christ is the Only Begotten Son of our Heavenly Father. We know that it is only through Him that we are redeemed. Because of this knowledge "we talk of Christ, we rejoice in Christ, we preach of Christ"[430] and we seek Him. We desire to know Him. We come unto Him. And we desire to bring others to Him.

At times our climbs may seem utterly overwhelming, but through Christ, He can take our distress and turn it into delight. I have come to know my Savior during the many climbs in my life. I have witnessed His light shine in my darkest hours. I have felt His presence near as I have sought Him. I have heard His voice as I have been still and listened. And I have recognized His love as I desired to know I was not alone.

If there is peace that is desired, I have discovered that it is found in Jesus Christ. If there is understanding needed, my experience has taught me that it is found in Jesus Christ. If there is hope wished for, I have learned that it is found in Jesus Christ. If there is light needed to guide our path, it is found in Jesus Christ because "Christ is our GPS—He will guide us successfully back home if we will but choose to follow Him."[431]

1. **Never doubt your own abilities**
2. **Our paths cross so we may lift one another**
3. **Keep taking small, simple, and faithful steps forward**
4. **Obey guidance and direction given by our prophets and apostles**
5. **Know you are a daughter of God with divine purpose and potential**
6. **Keep your focus on Jesus Christ**

---

[430] 2 Nephi 25:26, The Book of Mormon.
[431] Heise, Barbara A. "Grow Toward Christ." *BYU Speeches*, 2 Aug. 2010, speeches.byu.edu/talks/baraba-a-heise/grow-toward-christ/.

Equipped with the blessings of the knowledge we have received from the gospel of Jesus Christ our climbs in life may be easier, even if they don't always feel that way. Eventually, we will make it to the top of our mountains. Occasionally we will find ourselves walking through valleys, and at other times, through fields. And sometimes we climb one mountain only to find another steep climb awaiting us. If we continue forward with faith, continually seeking Christ, I know we will be guided and directed on our journeys.

I know this is true because we are women who have covenanted to follow Jesus Christ; we "know right from wrong"[432] and we "stand firm on the Lord's side, making choices that 'set [us] apart' from the rest of the world"[433] and we each have "a vital role, even a sacred mission to perform as a daughter in Zion."[434]

No matter your season in life, no matter your background or where you are on your journey, you are eternally loved, and you are "distinct and different—in happy ways—from the women of the world."[435]

A Japanese proverb says: *even specks of dust when piled together can become a mountain.*

I like to think the opposite: carrying just one speck of dust at a time, a mountain can be removed.

In the end, you will see that you are not just a mountain climber. YOU are a mountain mover! Even stone by stone, or pebble by pebble, or one speck of dust at a time, YOU are a mover of mountains!

The Lord needs women! The Lord has invited YOU! We are women who have the gift of the Holy Ghost, who receive personal

---

[432] Smoot, Mary E. "Rejoice Daughters of Zion," General Conference October 1999
[433] Ibid.
[434] Ibid.
[435] Kimball, Spencer W. "The Righteous Role of Women," General Conference October 1979

revelation, and who act on it. We are women who know our divine worth and who use the unmistakable gifts and talents we have been blessed with to stand up, speak up, and shine for the world to see! Our Savior, Jesus Christ, is the Light that each of us shines. The hope that keeps us faithfully moving forward. We are women who lift others, who encourage always, and who believe in Jesus Christ!

As a daughter of God, recognizably unique, unmistakably divine, you stand armed with knowledge, eternal attributes, and blessings from your Heavenly Father. You will not only climb your mountain you will absolutely conquer it!

Take your place and become the miracle that you *are* and watch as your mountains move!

This is YOUR time!

*Our Savior, Jesus Christ,
is the Light that each
of us shines. The hope
that keeps us faithfully
moving forward. We are
women who lift others,
who encourage always,
and who believe in
Jesus Christ!*

- Kay West -

This is
YOUR
time!

—12—
You

Your Message Here

Your Message Here

Your Message Here

Your Message Here

253

Your Message Here

Share your story with us
https://aworldwidesisterhood.com/book/

Author Biographies

in book chapter order

Starr Anderson

Starr currently lives in North Carolina with her husband, Robb, and seven of their eight children: ages 19, 18, 16, 14, 11, 10, 7 and 6 (Seven girls and one boy!) Her family is her everything! Starr is a native of California and has spent many years living in Utah. She has recently learned that you can love and cherish multiple places and the Lord can allow your heart to expand and make room for new friendships!

Starr served a full time mission for the Church of Jesus Christ of Latter-day Saints in Bilbao, Spain. She is a graduate of Brigham Young University with a Bachelor's Degree in Social Work. Early on in their marriage, Starr was able to use her degree and Spanish as she worked with battered women in a transitional housing unit. These skills have continued to be used throughout her life as she has served others.

Before graduating from BYU Starr earned her Associates Degree studying Fashion Design. The love of creating has always been a passion. Currently she owns a small business with her children which they have named "8 Stitches Through Time".

The name of this business is two fold; not only does it represent her love of sewing but it also plays off another passion, family relationships that span through time. Her love of family history has led to hundreds of hours of researching and discovering ancestors. The Lord has led Starr on a marvelous journey discovering her past.

Besides family, Starr's truest love is the scriptures and teaching and testifying of the truths found therein. This love came after her mission, while teaching at the MTC and helping write and pilot new curriculum about "likening the scriptures". Starr has had the opportunity to speak at several events, retreats, and conferences; including Brigham Young University's Women's Conference. Starr has also enjoyed being on a women's panel to answer questions about the beliefs of "Latter Day Saint Women" at a local university in North Carolina.

You can connect with Starr on Facebook @starrguyanderson

Chelsea
Bowen Bretzke

Chelsea Bowen Bretzke lives in Alberta, Canada where she loves hiking in the mountains, tends to over share on Instagram and frequently belts out Disney songs as she drives her 7 kids around in their huge 12 passenger van.

She loves traveling with her hubby, girls' nights, doing yoga and attending the temple. She hates cleaning bathrooms and thinks ordering groceries online is one the greatest blessings of the latter-days! But her favorite thing in the world is learning and teaching the gospel of Jesus Christ--whether that's to her cute primary class, or gospel doctrine; in a rowdy Come Follow Me lesson with her under appreciative kids or to young adults as a local institute teacher.

She especially seeks opportunities to connect with and empower women-- teaching Stake Relief Society scriptures classes; speaking at and organizing women's conferences; presenting firesides about Heavenly Mother or simply in a phone conversation with a friend-- there is nothing that thrills her spirit more than feeling the powerful doctrines of Christ healing and helping individual hearts take courage and know who they truly are.

You can connect with Chelsea on her blog at bretzke.blogspot.com or on Instagram @chelseabelleb

Renee Alberts

Renee grew up a member of the Church of Jesus Christ of Latter-Day Saints. She was born and raised in Auckland, New Zealand and lived there until being sealed to her eternal companion in the Hamilton New Zealand Temple, 11 years ago; and moved to her husband's homeland of Australia. Renee is a devoted mother of 5 young children. She studied and graduated from her Undergraduate and Masters Degrees (in Education) as a mature-aged student, with her first three children in tow. Renee is a creative who loves music, hand lettering and watercolor art.

Renee created Inspiring Women Who Know (IWWK) in October 2018. It has been a passion project that she has been guided to develop gradually through the years, "line upon line". IWWK focuses on drawing closer to the Savior through faith in Him, knowing our divine worth and developing our awareness to hear the voice of the Lord in our individual lives. Renee believes that learning to receive personal revelation is a journey of a lifetime, but as our spirit becomes more in tune with our divine nature, our confidence to hear Him increases.

Renee is a content contributor at A Worldwide Sisterhood.

You can connect with Renee on Instagram @inspiringwomenwhoknow or at aworldwidesisterhood.com or on Instagram @aworldwidesisterhood

Darla Trendler

Darla Trendler is the creator and host of the Spiritually Minded Women podcast (formerly Spiritually Minded Mom) where she helps Latter-day Saint women embrace their personal and unique journey on the covenant path. She is also the creator of an online course, *The Latter-day Mom's Guide to Spiritually Empowering Your Teen* and has been a speaker at several in person and online conferences. Her goal is to help women gain confidence in hearing and following God's voice. Since childhood, Darla has had a love of the scriptures and finds great strength from the examples of the people she reads about. As a young adult, she served as a missionary in Ohio and has since served at church as a teacher and leader of youth and children.

Darla's current stage of life involves watching her four children leave home, having teenagers, and being her kids' biggest cheerleader. Darla works with her husband in their car business and when she has a spare minute, she enjoys weightlifting and writing in her journal. She and her family love living in the Arizona desert and you can frequently find them spending time together boating or having pushup competitions.

You can connect with Darla at spirituallymindedwomen.com or on Instagram @spirituallymindedwomen

Audra Elkington

Audra lives in North Carolina with her husband and three children - ages 13, 10 and 5. She is a graduate of Brigham Young University with a Bachelor's degree in Psychology. She has put that degree to good use as she has navigated the long, windy road of parenting children with mental health challenges.

Audra loves inspiring others through public speaking and writing. She uses her own personal experiences to help others find examples of the Lord's hand in their own lives. She has been featured on several podcasts, including This is the Gospel and Spiritually Minded Mom. She has written articles for communities such as Work + Wonder and A Worldwide Sisterhood. Audra was also a local presenter at Time Out for Women where she shared her journey of leaving the Church of Jesus Christ of Latter-day Saints and how God helped her find her way back.

In 2019, Audra founded and hosted a retreat for Christian women in North Carolina which allowed her to combine some of her favorite passions –unity, friendship and developing personal relationships with the Savior.

Audra is the content manager and creative director at A Worldwide Sisterhood.

You can connect with Audra on Instagram @audraelkington and Facebook @audraelkington or at aworldwidesisterhood.com or on Instagram @aworldwidesisterhood

Lauren Madsen

Lauren Madsen is a photo-taking, scrapbook-making, kindergarten teacher turned stay-at-home mom of two girls and two boys. She met her husband Christopher in physical science class at Brigham Young University. They have been married for seventeen years.

Lauren loves reading, writing poetry, family history work, spending time outside with her kids, and Friday night dates with her husband. The mountains are her happy place, but she has discovered a similar peace right on her own front porch.

Over the years, Lauren has found joy in serving as a team member for The Small Seed and committee member for The Festival of Trees. Lauren currently works as a member of the SALT Gathering team. If there is one thing she is most passionate about, it is Christ's teaching: "Let your light so shine before men, that they may see your good works, and glorify your Father which is in heaven" (Matthew 5:16). Lauren hopes to inspire others that through love, service and record-keeping, we have the opportunity to point others to the Savior, creating a light that lingers long after this life.

You can connect with Lauren on Instagram @a.lingering.light

Jodi L Nicholes

Jodi grew up in a small town where life is simple, and the love is big. As a child vocal prodigy, Jodi's professional music career began at the tender age of ten years old. She found herself singing and performing for thousands on the stages of Las Vegas, Nevada. In an industry that places value and worth on external validation, Jodi found herself in a state of confusion.

This led Jodi on a journey of self-discovery to better understand her divine identity and inherent worth. Jodi has dedicated the past twenty-five years and over twelve thousand hours to learning, researching, implementing, and teaching thousands of women and girls how to cultivate their divine nature. Jodi has a gift for seeing the bigger picture and discovering eternal truths in the seemly small moments of each day. She believes it's in these moments God whispers, I see you, I hear you, and you are loved!

Jodi is an award-winning vocalist whose music is heard on radio stations across the globe. These days most of Jodi's performances take place in her kitchen, singing and dancing with her kids. Aside from Jodi's music career, she is a writer, speaker, and Educator. Jodi's family is her most prized possession. She resides in Lindon, Utah, with her husband and three children.

You can connect with Jodi at thewomenwhoshine.com or on Instagram @womenwhoshine

Becky Squire

Becky Squire was born and raised in Ogden, Utah. She met her husband, Josh, at Weber State University and they have been married since 2003. Their relationship can be described as soulmates who are complete opposites! They have 4 amazing kids: Ian, Amelia, Eli, and Bronx.

Becky enjoys running, especially in the mountains of Northern Utah (but any mountain will do). She loves to travel with her family and National Parks have become a family favorite. Becky also enjoys baking and is a self-proclaimed cheesecake connoisseur.

Becky is the founding editor of Latter-day Woman Magazine and has a passion for mentoring women who feel called to righteously influence the world online. Becky has been published in the Ensign, LDS Living, The Today Show, a variety of media websites.

You can connect with Becky at beckysquire.com on Instagram @beckysquire or Facebook @beckysquireblog

Or at latterdaywomanmagazine.com or on
Instagram@latterdaywoman and Facebook @latterdaywoman

Tiffany Fletcher

Tiffany Fletcher, author of *Mother Had a Secret*, *It's a Light Thing!*, and *The Trouble with Charity*, is the second oldest of six children, born to a mother diagnosed with Multiple Personalities, now known as Dissociative Identity Disorder. Because of her mother's illness, Tiffany often faced the nightmare of an abusive male alter and her mother's prescription drug addiction. Yet, through it all, Tiffany faced her circumstances with courage and the ability to see the good.

It was her belief in God and her love of writing and music that helped Tiffany cope with the difficulties of her childhood and offered her peace amidst the chaos. Seeing the good in every situation, and especially the good in her mother, became the hope that brought Tiffany from a place of darkness to incredible light and love. As an author and inspirational speaker, Tiffany loves sharing her story and inspiring others to find resilience and peace in their own lives.

Tiffany loves God, adores Jesus, and is a lover of all things light. She is fiercely devoted to her family and enjoys spending lazy days with her amazing husband and five incredible children.

Tiffany also cherishes relationships and values connecting with others.

If you would like to connect with her, you can follow her inspirational thoughts on Facebook @tiffanyyoungfletcher or Instagram @tiffnyfletcher, read her blog or listen to a podcast at itsalightthing.org, watch her story or book her for a speaking event at tiffanyfletcher.me, or email her directly at authortiffanyfletcher@gmail.com.

Rhonda Steed

Rhonda is a life-long member of the Church of Jesus Christ of Latter-day Saints thanks to her parents joining the church when they were younger. Rhonda was married to her love, Regan, in 2000 and together they have 5 unique, creative, incredibly smart kids: Alden (17), Lucy (14), Eli (11), Oliver (8) and Norah (7). They have a chaotic fun home where lots of noise is made, books are read and creative messes are made. They love music in their house of all kinds (really except Rap) from the different lessons her kids take to the various basement concerts they host.

Rhonda likes to pretend she's organized, but really, she's an unorganized, spontaneous, creative extrovert. She's interested in learning everything and seeing everywhere and anywhere. She's a bit obsessed with bread (in fact a "bread head") and she loves baking and cooking anything, especially if it is difficult to bake. She loves pretty much all good food and her husband teases her that she's a food snob but she'll kindly accept any treats you want to make her.

Rhonda is a professional photographer, a for-fun painter, an obsessive memory keeper, a quick reader, and a lover of nature. She will talk to pretty much anyone and loves making new friends and considers herself great at friend matching – helping match people who would be good friends with each other.

Rhonda is terrible at saying no to things so she's currently sitting on four town boards in her lovely town of Raymond, Alberta, Canada. She loves to discuss the different aspects of the gospel and currently serves as a ward gospel doctrine teacher.

Rhonda is the digital illustrator and content contributor at A Worldwide Sisterhood.

You can connect with Rhonda on Instagram @iamrhondasteed or @rhondasteedphotography and Facebook @rhonda.steedr or at aworldwidesisterhood.com or on Instagram @aworldwidesisterhood.

Kay West

Kay is the founder and creator of *A Worldwide Sisterhood* and *Distinct and Different*, and the creator of #liftwomensevents, #5days5women, and #testimoniesofChrist. She is sealed to her very best friend for over 21 years and is the mother of two children.

Kay deeply loves her Savior, Jesus Christ. She has gained her own testimony of Him through life experiences, study, faith, personal revelation, and striving to seek Him daily. She believes in her sacred roles of wife and mother, and in her divine purpose as a daughter of God.

Kay has been invited to speak at many events, has contributed to several blogs and articles, and has been interviewed on several podcasts. She is the author of a few books, and she loves to support her children in their business raising awareness and kindness for children with special needs.

Kay is a speaker, author, a great listener, and a wonderful supporter of all women faithfully navigating their way through this crazy thing called life.

You can connect with Kay at aworldwidesisterhood.com or on Instagram @aworldwidesisterhood. Connect with Kay's children quietlybeingkind.com or on Instagram @quietlybeingkind.

A Worldwide Sisterhood

aworldwidesisterhood.com
Instagram @aworldwidesisterhood
email: info@aworldwidesisterhood.com

Made in the USA
Las Vegas, NV
21 December 2023

83298747R00164